The Beach of Morning

The Beach of Morning

A Walk in West Africa

Stephen Pern

HODDER AND STOUGHTON
LONDON SYDNEY AUCKLAND TORONTO

British Library Cataloguing in Publication Data
Pern, Stephen
   The beach of morning.
   1. Africa, West—Description and travel—1951–
   I. Title
   916.6'04   DT472

   ISBN 0 340 26236 2

Hodder and Stoughton Editorial Office: 47 Bedford Square, London WC1B 3DP.

For Jeremy and Sue

Illustrations

between pages 112–13

First steps★
First camp★
The lake creeping up on Waz
Shua herd
Kanuri girl selling milk
Three sisters
Trouble with the donkeys★
Waz and Claude
An old Waa clansman
The Maiden of the Mandaras
Fatima of the fish camp
The Rockosaurs
A headload of sorghum
Traditional Vomengu dress★
Florence Nightingale strikes again★
Waz unpacking
Borroro youth
Borroro woman
Young Borroro girl
Wafundumta's wife
Crossing the Benue

Photographs by Stephen Pern, except those marked with an asterisk which are by Waziri Amadu.

Maps

Eastern Nigeria and the Cameroons   24
North East Bornu   66
The Mandara Mountains   156
Tribal areas of North East Nigeria   207

Thanks

I was sitting in Mombasa post office, dredging my brain for things to say on postcards that, with a bit of luck, might beat me back to England, when my eyes fell on the desk. Etched into the blotter was the following testament to the agony of writing:

SNORGITNG
SW &
SNORGEEWG
SNORKLING

I have to thank the population of Nigeria for sparing me such problems with the present book. I hope that *The Beach of Morning* will express the debt I owe to them and to their land.

To Waziri, Jalo and Michel go the thanks of a traveller to his companions. Waz's relatives, particularly Mairama Mubi and Idrissu Madugu, were very generous with their hospitality as were Garba Yusuf Sadek, Jan Brown, Gloria and Laurel, Tim Langford and Nikos Louridas. The advice and information I received from Christine Betterton, Tony Akisole and Phil Hall were invaluable while Joanna Barlow gave some memorable Hausa lessons. For their extraordinary kindness in nursing me back to health Hanni and the Quark family will always have my gratitude, as will Bob and Nan Wedderburn who also helped me so very much whenever I descended on them.

The anthropologist Walter van Beek was an unwitting sounding board for some of the ideas expressed in this book, and the help of Christine Hammerschmitt and Anne-Laure Lagron in translating various works from German and French was also much appreciated. Dr. G. Wickens and his colleagues at Kew helped with the botanical problems, and Hazel Roberts of the School of Oriental and African Studies library was ever obliging. Henry Cass made some very useful comments on the manuscript, and Mrs. R. M. Harris and Jane Adams spent long hours deciphering my curious scrawl. I must also thank Maggie Body for her skilful editing.

Finally I would like to thank my mother, brother and sister-in-law for putting up with me while I was in my garret.

S. P.

Traveller, you must set out
At dawn. And wipe your feet upon
The dog-nose wetness of the earth.

from *Death in the Dawn* by Wole Soyinka

1

Jan and I drove Waziri up to Heathrow in mid-September. I had just had a cholera shot and was feeling exceedingly grotty, despite having taken the "air" in nearby Staines when we stopped to buy a watch for Waz's father. Now, in the mephitic atmosphere of Terminal Three, I craved the relative fragrance of the South Circular, and so we left Waziri to it. Jan drove the car back to Hastings while I felt sick in the back. The border project was under way.

The plan was to cross West Africa on foot from the Sahara desert to the Atlantic Ocean. From Lake Chad in the north, Waz and I hoped to follow the border country between Nigeria and the Cameroons, first crossing the open, semi-arid savannahs, then winding down through the Mandara Mountains to the River Benue. Continuing south we would enter some fairly remote country on the edge of the Mambilla Plateau, cross the plateau itself, and descend to the high forest and thick jungle of the Cameroons. As a finale I wanted to nip up the north face of Mount Cameroon then come down the other side to reach Victoria on the coast, making a total distance of roughly a thousand miles.

The borders project was not my first visit to Africa. In 1977 I walked round a lake in Kenya, a journey of about four hundred miles, and before that I had already spent two years as a game preservation officer in northern Nigeria. I absorbed a little Hausa in that time but it had, unfortunately, dribbled from my sieve-like memory. I had therefore been revising diligently during the summer period while posing as an instructor at an Outward Bound school on the Celtic fringe. I practised daily on the oleaginous apprentices entrusted to my care. They would very sportingly yell out appropriate phrases through the claggy mists of Cader Idris, alarming the sheep but impressing the tourists who naturally took us for a group of exhausted bards, yodelling for help in Welsh.

"Hope Waz'll be OK," said Jan, as we sped home along the Sevenoaks by-pass.

"No problem," I said, "he's nineteen and he is Nigerian after all." He was flying home by way of Lagos airport, a severe enough test of a travelling man's moral fibre, and held by many to be as strongly encouraging of hairs on the thorax as, say, a capsize in the Southern Ocean or a tumble on the face of Everest. I personally was flying to Kano.

Waziri had won a scholarship to England at the age of twelve. He had returned to the fairly remote area of north-eastern Nigeria from which he came every second summer but, despite such infrequent contact, he had retained a strong desire to go back for good when his studies were finished. His father was a subsistence farmer and petty trader, but through his mother's family he was related to men of some local influence. He had already left his Bexhill school and was halfway through a course in agricultural engineering when we had met and, since my plans for the border project coincided with his for returning home, we thought that we might do the thing together.

I had the money and Waz had the knowledge. His years in England had given him a rare fluency in two very different cultures and I hoped that he might act as a sort of bridge, enabling my mind to enter Africa on more than purely physical terms. Waz was fluent in English, Hausa and Fulani, the three most widely spoken languages in northern Nigeria, as well as in his tribal tongue, Marghi, which would be invaluable to us when we reached the Mandara Mountains. My "plume de ma tante" stammerings would see us through the Francophone Cameroons. Between us we had the most important languages but with over three hundred others spoken within her borders, Nigeria is the sort of country where the tower of Babel might well have been taken for a multi-storey car park. Were the

14

tower ever to be rebuilt a Nigerian company would almost certainly land the contract.

Waziri was flying out three weeks before me in order to greet his family before the great trek began. I planned to arrive in early October, when the rains would be more or less over. With a generous allowance for the unforeseen, always a good move in West Africa, I reckoned that we might start the walk by late October and follow the dry season as it advanced slowly south. Before leaving England, however, I caught the heebie-jeebies. The heebies had first struck on an abortive trip to Tanzania and I knew the symptoms—hands like sweating glycerine, lead shot in the stomach, a sahara of a tongue, scattered and despairing thoughts and little to say but sighs. When shorts were long and hair was short and chaps got into funks I suppose I would have shot myself or joined the Foreign Legion. I did not exactly understand the cause, but it had to do with doubt. A letter came from Waziri. It read like a suicide note and covered his expensive extrication from Lagos airport, cholera epidemics in the hills, possible marriage (his) and desperate exchange rates. I had to get a grip and I needed a few good omens.

The spirit of that very day was one omen, with an autumnal wind of lofty blue, fresh as new split conkers. Pigging it on wholemeal chocolate biscuits, Jan and I headed for Jevington in the South Downs. Out of curiosity I ducked into the parish church, a little dank for such a day, and I read the memorials set into the walls. I am sure that one of them was my second omen. "Sacred to the memory of George Thomas Basden," it read, "Rector of Jevington . . . 1936–1944 . . . missionary in Nigeria 1900–1935 and Archdeacon of the Niger." Two-thirds of the border project followed through the eastern borderlands of Nigeria. I hoped that the Reverend Basden might approve.

We walked uphill towards the flossy clouds on short, un-obtrusive grass. It was a day of breathless clarity. We drifted on, following the crewcut turf over the chalky cranium of Windover Hill, the Vale of Sussex blowing straight into our pupils. The victuals were finished. Being afternoon, the creamy thought of buns set in and we went down to Alfriston for tea. Politely satisfied we started back towards the car, following the Cuckmere river. A lady and a gentleman were walking towards us along the other bank, and the lady waved as they passed by. She said later that she had liked the look of us. Jan waved back, but she is Irish. Being a mere Englishman myself I was having a tussle with my inhibitions. I thought that I knew the man, but the meeting seemed too providential. It is amazing how much effort it sometimes takes to open one's mouth. I only had to shout across the muddy water but I felt about as tongue-tied as a swain at a ball. I briefly considered jumping in. How pathetic.

"Excuse me," I eventually shouted, "is your name Hillaby?"

"It is."

"Ah. Hallo. You may not remember me. I'm the bloke who wrote the book about Lake Rudolph. You wrote the foreword."

"My friend!"

After lots more tea, and even beer, we dropped them at the London train. I had had a champagne of a day with omens enough for any wobbling expeditionary.

Motive.

I've always had a misty sense that using machines is somehow cheating. As a child I faintly resented living in a house: I felt at home down by our stream, among the phantom crocodiles. I tried my hand at making flint tipped arrows, and it took some time to reconcile myself to using rifles, even though I had never shot a thing with bows or catapults. I questioned socks in summer time and ties throughout the year. At school a man had once shown slides of aborigines. They impressed me in a way that neither Bankers nor Butchers nor Sportsmen nor Spacemen ever had; though still in shorts, I had sensed these possibilities to be simply variations on a theme with which I was not in complete accord. I had never felt any desperate urge to Man the Barricades, Shoot Peasants, Missionise, or Make my Mark, but grew up vaguely uneasy at the prospect of a sweatless and soft handed life. I had no illusions about the dignity of manual labour, but worried gently in regions which, as I later discovered, were loosely signposted "Alienation" and "The Division of Labour".

I went to university a little out of fear, and remained there ill at ease except on summer wanderings. Those summer days offered direct choice and daily changing circumstance which I, alone and footloose, could master. Two years of intense boy scouting in Nigeria again put off immersion in, quite what, I seldom wondered. I had lived where aboriginal fantasies had had full reign and I became a species of conscientious objector to orthodoxy. I came to see life as a bran tub, worth dipping into for "the experience", and assumed that the alternative was to regard life as a shooting gallery in which one took aim at a preselected target.

And what had those days in Africa been like? Some were, of course, pure treacle, but others sliced a perfect bow wave, stiff with dolphins. I worked for the wildlife services of two northern states and quickly dispensed with servants, tents and boiled water. In consequence I had diarrhoea each time I returned from the bush and was often very lonely, but my style of life became quite flexible. I ended up on a lorry-load of peppers with a couple of Libyans. We drove to Tindouf in western Algeria and tried to sell the peppers. It was 1973. I had a narrow squeak with someone else's marijuana at a Spanish customs post and puked incessantly from Dieppe across to Newhaven. In the time away I had achieved a sympathy with space and heat, although I had not been greatly fond of feeling for ever foreign.

Recapture old sensations? No, I think not. It's more fun to launch new boats than to winch up what has sunk.

2

The day came, grey and cold. I fed the cat and cut a bunch of lavender. An old friend took me to the station. The summer had at last collapsed.

Sussex rolled quite smoothly into Kent, both counties now mellowing from fruitfulness to open rot. The still air had in it the muted blue-grey of pigeons' wings, suspended wet and dead until the dignifying rigor of first frosts came down to lay the ghosts of summer. Old sheep merged with the dirty stubble, knocking soggy thistles down and laddering the spiders' webs.

The ridged disaster of a potato field went clattering by and, beyond, above an orchard, white oast cowls struck boldly through the haze. Apples dripped like rosy children from a maze of leafless twigs. A golf course sped by in winks behind an elegant frieze of birch, but elsewhere the trackside flora degenerated steadily to mongrel weeds. We entered jobbing builder land, with, at first, back yards and garden sheds, and then spare lots and fenced off bits for greyhounds and container trucks—the sparse prairies of London town. The train rocked on towards a range of tower blocks and chimneys and a snowy glimpse of St. Paul's dome; then in we went, four storeys up above the barge-grey Thames and, "Charing Cross, all change!".

"Take a good cigarette, Mr. Gentleman, you see, the best." Sitting next to me, a stubby finger traces golden letters, long and tall like prison bars. The man's original home was Srinagar and twenty years in Burnley hardly show. He is still a good Muslim, and, with money saved from trading blue jeans round the northern markets, here he is, excited, free, and flying off to Mecca. As the tobacco burns I am thinking about his dreams of Paradise and I silently demolish his foreign scheme of things. My final puff, in turn, incinerates this absurd tendency of mine to judge what is not in court. I crumble the butt and listen to my neighbour talking of Kashmir.

The Third World slurps you up inside the Cairo transit hall, with men on jobs that buttons do in Europe. The men salute and call you "sir" despite dry taps and loos crammed tight with reject origami. Waiting overnight I shared a room with Colin, out to see his folks on contract up in Sokoto. The sheets were limp as flannels and my feet were exploring for cool patches when the morning came.

"Hello, old friend," said Colin, wrinkling his nose. He was talking to his shirt which, being unclean, had not slept well. Nor had I, and smiling like an otter I rolled again into the surf which throws up dreams along the beach of morning. I conjured up our cat stretched out on warm dry garden stones. Jan was sewing in the sun while I commanded alterations to my gear. I drifted back into a Welsh July and smelt the sea and heard the tide which sucked at priceless moonlight shattered on the sand. Tethered boats swung at their moorings and the wind drove in a massive cloud bank off the Irish Sea, firmly investing the moon and banging shut the box of night. A few lights shone like periscopes across the smothered estuary and caught the monster Dovey slipping out from Wales into the sea.

The flight to Kano was uneventful and happened in the dark. We landed and, following Colin off the plane, a little raspberry caught my eye, embroidered small upon a splendid tit. The words "Confiture de Framboise" were stitched in neatly underneath. A rhythmic swell heaved at the pendulous fruit while bustling squalls of "we're-off-first" thrashed past. She sat Madonna-like, her baby sunk serenely on the mattress of her thighs. What luck, I thought, to have a mum who feeds you raspberry milkshakes.

I walked towards the lights where customs men were waiting, and so, I fervently hoped, was Waz. Travelling with a partner was going to be a novelty. I usually set out on journeys by myself, like the driver of an empty car, with lots of space for picking people up along the way. I would not have such freedom with a partner to consider and, consideration not being my strong suit, I would have to adapt. I was unused to entering consultations over the petty details of life and anxious that Waz and I clicked on the daily round. I was also wary of the subtle dilutions which can wash travellers caught within a bubble of consensus but, at the very least, I felt in Waz's company that I had an extra sense organ, if not, as yet, a friend. We both knew that the spark of friendship had not struck, for which, in a way, I was glad. The absence of great warmth in our relationship would allow us both a certain independence of each other.

A dark red fuel truck scattered us within the lit half-acre of the terminal. Waz was bouncing lightly through converging sprays of passengers.

"That's him, I'm OK now," I said, and Colin said, "Oh, good."

Brittle, brass winged grasshoppers were flaring round the customs shed like windmills stuck in overdrive. The shadeless neon pulled them in from humid night. Since the ceiling fans were all gathering dust, the insects' only danger lay from lizards waiting coldly on the floor. The human scrummage was too occupied to worry about scuttle, snap and murder at its feet.

"Excuse me, you are Mister Colin? Give your passport, and that of your brother too." A man took the documents and moled his way up to the plywood counter. He said he was the driver for Colin's father but we marked him nonetheless. He stood on tiptoe, waving like a child at royalty through a hedge of arms to raise attention and a stamp. Although the uniforms behind the counter shone with starch and elbow grease, the wooden desks and barriers were oddly crude. The signs all looked homemade and painted in a rush, the sort of things which advertise brown eggs and rhubarb far down country lanes. Instructions were in any case ignored completely by the queue, a feral, chaos-begins-in-Calais sort of queue, which the Swiss would call a riot. The sweating driver wriggled free and led us through to new anxieties within the luggage hall. I sat and smoked until the Mountain Mule, my greenish rucksack, fell and crushed some weaker bags already off the trolleys dragged in from the night. A squiggling chalk approached and made its mark. I joined Waz at the entrance and we took a taxi to the house of his friend Garba Yusuf.

Garba Yusuf's father dealt in tyres and had been to Mecca. His name was Alhaji Yusuf Garba. We drove into the family courtyard rather gingerly, avoiding shoals of Hondas and a Peugeot pick-up truck. Two storeys of breeze blocks and cement rose above us like a private block of flats. I stumbled up an irregular concrete staircase to a balcony and followed Waz into the glow of Garba's television (monstrous wrestlers from America). The dozen watchers hardly stirred but Garba was effusive.

"Welcome, you are welcome," Garba said, "in fact."

Turning from the porcine phosphorescence, Garba led us through into his bedroom where we dumped the gear and said hallo, again "in fact", I noticed. A short power cut broke the ice and as the light returned another friend called Ali Abdullahi introduced himself.

"Hi, Stephen," he said, "how's it going, get yourself a little rest." He had made a pilgrimage of sorts himself, not to Mecca but to Tennessee, where he had just qualified as a medical technician. Now he was a "been-to", been to overseas that is. Garba was waiting to go. His father had not yet arranged a scholarship.

21

"You take your wash," Garba said, and as the taps were dry he sent a boy to bring a bucket from the tank. The bathroom was totally uncluttered. Besides the fittings and the grey concrete walls the room was furnished with a bar of soap, a flannel and a quantity of grime. No lino, no linen, no smells in jars, neither rubber ducks nor hanging plants intruded. No plugs or mugs or homilies, nor bath hats, bath salts, bath mats—the simplicity of the village hut persisted despite the new materials of its construction. Other than the unremarkable furniture, some forlorn and plastic lily-of-the-valley and the titillating cover of a paperback by James Hadley Chase were all that broke what, to a European observer, was the cultural silence of the sitting room. To a Nigerian, however, those things said, "Hallo, we were bought at Kingsway stores, the biggest shop in town and whoever bought us knows his way around a supermarket—impressive, huh?" I have calabashes displayed on my walls at home, which, to West African eyes, is a bit like hanging up the washing-up bowl, but which, to Europeans, say, "Hi, we're just a spot of ethnographic detail, Stephen's been to AFRICA." When two cultures meet it is as well to admit that, far from knowing each other's code books, we may not even recognise the signalling stations. The real furniture in Garba's room was still immersed in the aural candy floss pouring from the television.

I needed some cigarettes and passed back down the roughcast stairs and out into the streets. The maigardi, or nightwatchman, stirred on his mat, retrieved an arm from somewhere in his robes and shook his fist respectfully, the Hausa equivalent of a tug at the forelock. "Ranka ya dade," he mumbled, which means, roughly, "A long life to you, Sor." Like most maigardis he was built on the lines of a radio mast, wore a veil, and having slept all day to prepare himself for the dark watches, slept all night as well. His ancestors had probably spent the bulk of their waking hours planning and executing raids on the very people he was now supposed to be protecting. The Tamashek and Tuareg of what is now the republic of Niger

22

were once a major threat to the city states of Hausaland and had, with others, almost brought the empire of Bornu to its knees by the time Europeans arrived in force at the end of the nineteenth century. The droughts of the 1970s severely disrupted the social and economic life of the northern pastoralists and Nigeria's vibrant economy has attracted them south. These tall, robed figures, disdainful of physical work, are a common sight throughout Nigeria—a diaspora of redundant knights, reduced to games of snap in the proletarian dust of the towns.

The wide, rutted pavements were, in daylight, extensions of the shops and businesses behind them, though at this hour even the outer fringe of stallholders had wrapped up shop in dusty polythene and gone, leaving the night to street hawkers and their sooty lamps. These boys were the bipedal equivalent of a village store and carried their trinkets and sundries in bundles on their heads, Rubik Cubes of petty trade built with immense skill and bound with strips of rubber. Garba caught me up as I was paying for my cigarettes. He was a little hurt that I had tried to buy them for myself. He made me take my money back, paid, and gave me the change. I was a guest, but having only just arrived I would be some time in slipping round my cultural skin.

I woke to a two-stroke chorus buzzing past outside. Kano was well on its way to work when Garba brought in a tray of bread and bowls of sweet gruel made from guinea corn. We then throttled out to join the flow of Japanese technology and drove to Kano market. Waz had borrowed a couple of motor-bikes and I rode pillion behind Garba who sailed neatly into the ranks of bikes flung up against the main gate. He chose a minder from the swarming throng whose business was to park, protect and polish all the chrome. Escaping the insistent solicitations of prospective guides and porters we worked our way down the first alleyway.

You can buy single cigarettes in Kano market, or, if you wish, a barrow full of leaf and plaited coils of dark and

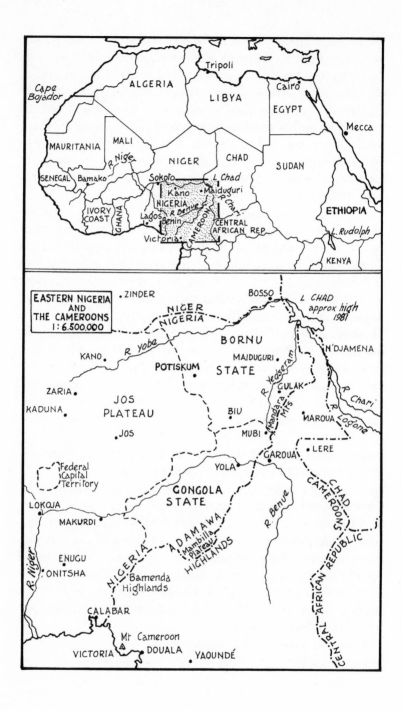

tangy twist. You can get individual needles or truckloads of scrap, eggs or butchered camels. Pirated cassettes are stacked in teetering columns on the backs of bicycles. Men sell cinnamon and stereos, rice and the ingredients for charms. They offer amber and gum arabic, gold and black eyed beans. The senses bathe in treats of ginger, drains and meat, fruit and fragrant spices. Old beggars call down blessings over booming disco sounds and people are rushing, crushing everywhere. Rich man, Poor man, Beggar man, Thief; Silk, Satin, Cotton, Rags; Lepers, Cripples and Calculators. A thousand prices and a thousand voices. Life in Africa is a contact sport.

Nigerians used to travel here and there in vivid clusters, stuck like jolly swarms of bees all over ancient Mammy Wagons. These miracles of bodge and paint still trundle by arthritically, odd-jobbing on the modern roads unrolled like tarmac carpet through the bush, but most people go by Peugeot taxi now, or by minibus.

Garba and his friend took Waz and me to the Kano lorry park, a seething mass of cars and anxious people trying to fill them up. Yelling "Bornu" loudly, we were quickly rustled through the crowd to a long distance taxi needing only us to fill its complement of six passengers. I settled back upon the plastic seat, soon dripping with my sweat, and watched the mesmerising sameness of savannah streaming by the whole way to Maiduguri. The different zones of vegetation in Nigeria run roughly east to west and so to get much variation one has to travel north and south, like the annual rain clouds coming from the sea. Most of the country is below five thousand feet, but few countries in tropical Africa have such a range of vegetation types, varying from rain forest in the south-east to dry thorn savannah vegetation round Lake Chad.

The taxi driver ran a Christian enterprise, by name the Blessed Emmanuel Express. Flagged down just east of Potiskum he stopped to fill a vacant seat. A peasant hitched his robe and garbled toothless Kanuri through the window. Virtually no one speaks the Kanuri language outside Bornu and Kanuri speakers tend to be conservative, unlike their fellow countrymen who are amazing linguists. The peasant's destination remained a mystery despite the driver's fairly simple line of questioning.

"Where?" was all the driver said.

He said it several times. Then, pointing to the old man's tightly closed hand he shouted, "Money!"

Fingers like upholstered sausages bloomed hesitantly, revealing coins worth roughly half a furlong as the taxi flies. We drove off abruptly.

October in Bornu is hot and humid with vagrant rain clouds still about, due to the southward migration of the Intertropical Convergence Front. This is not a political organisation but an atmospheric boundary between monsoonal and continental air masses. In Nigeria it is the south-west monsoon, which, having brought the summer rains from the sea, is pushed south again by a hot, dry, northerly air stream known as the harmattan. This knowledge is of little comfort to the wilting newcomer who by midday begins to feel that rigor mortis might be fun. Sweating it out in the taxi I invented a new verb. To letharge: a process of trans-migration whereby the soul of a nematode enters the crisp and keen young human body and reduces it to a mass of wet Kleenex.

Waz and I did it for 350 miles all the way from Kano, unpeeling in the capital of Bornu, Maiduguri, where I left my passport with a friend of a friend in the hope that an extension to my one month visitor's visa might be forthcoming. We then found more transport and continued south for three more hours to Waz's home village of Gulak.

Intercity travel in Nigeria happens at average speeds in excess of sixty miles an hour, an advantage of the long straight roads and the relatively light traffic. The disadvantage is that accidents are frequent and horrific. Unlike their South American counterparts who may lack caution but tend to be skilful, the Nigerian driver lacks more or less everything but a burning desire to fly. The pedestrian population is not yet accustomed to traffic and the predominantly bovine animal population is large, unfenced, and unpredictable. If you're tired of life, the saying goes, drive Nigeria.

3

There was a delay of nineteen days before Waz and I actually began our walk. Waz had first to escort his sister to her new school down in the city of Benin, and a public holiday followed for which he wanted to be in Gulak. I used the time to visit Yola, the capital of Gongola state, and Maiduguri again. I bought as many maps as I could, made certain financial arrangements, and I renewed the few contacts I still had after an eight year gap. A friendly wildlife officer took me to the Bornu state fisheries department which maintains an establishment on Lake Chad within three miles of the Niger border. I was given a kind letter of introduction asking for "all assistance and a boat", which, although I did not know it at the time, reflected a certain ignorance of the situation at the fishing department's front line. I was also warned about the disturbed "security situation" in the lake region and was told to watch out for police and army patrols.

"Just pass yourselves off as Greeks," said my adviser, "there's loads of them up there stumbling about the bush for Edok-Eta, the irrigation people."

I had a date one evening at the Maiduguri club. I am not a member and asked the gateman in his sentry box if I could go on to the verandah and wait.

"No," he said, with the characteristically numb indifference of Nigerian petty employees dealing with the general public. I had experienced the same thing at the post office that afternoon. Brushing through an outer cordon of chaps selling magazines and cigarettes, I had side-stepped the lepers clogging up the door, but bounced straight off a group in the hall who appeared to be giving an impromptu performance of the honey bees'

28

pollen dance. A drone sat idling but unmoved on his stool behind a wire grille, chatting casually with a mate. He looked about fifteen. Battered folders holding stamps were laid enticingly upon the desk. He turned towards the buzzing mob, gently swinging his legs and ripping off the perforated margins which stuck out between the leaves.

"Yes?"

"Two 30 kobo stamps, please."

"Stamps?" Long silence. Looks very uninvolved. Fiddles with the battered folders. "No stamps."

The pressure grew as customers piled up.

"No stamps?" Absolute silence, except for that ripping sound of little perforations. Not a flicker of explanation from the mask of arrogance and blind ignorance behind the desk. I could have ripped into it, smashed it in, but lightly ground my teeth instead. The youth got up and walked away. His friend sat down in his place. The youth wasn't even an employee. Just popped in to incense the public, I supposed.

"Yes?" the actual clerk had said after arranging his paraphernalia at some length.

"Two 30 kobo stamps, please."

"Stamps," echoed the clerk with absolute neutrality. He too began the perforation routine. Why the mental hospitals weren't full I could not imagine.

"Yes, stamps," I said, waving a small note. The clerk wore an air of studied decision making. Should he really run for President? Was a distinction between culture and society valid? Should he read more Levi-Strauss? I would never know.

"No change," he said. I gave up.

Waiting outside the Maiduguri club I noticed a sign above me which said, "Unaccompanied children are not allowed in the club premises at all times." The same seemed to apply to adults. I occupied myself with the club notice board. "Warning," it said,

The management committee of the Lake Chad Club, Maiduguri, wishes to inform all members that it takes a very serious view of behaviour unbecoming of the status of the club, and irregularities in non-payment of subscriptions due from members . . . defaulting members will be liable to suspension and in extreme cases to dismissal . . . we have a standard to maintain in this society . . .

The colonial administration left its own version of the English language to Nigeria. One does not expel a member from a club, one "dismisses" him. In this sense the inertia and rigidity of civil service life transfers itself to the national consciousness. Teachers do not "teach at" a certain school, they are "posted" there. People are not "in" or "out", they are either "on seat" or "on tour". One does not have a job, one has a post or a position. The inability to disassociate the structures of official-dom from the realities of actual life was neatly encapsulated in the other notice on the board.

For your information the Club Election is approaching to elect another committee of the club to power. So therefore any member that doesn't pay up to date would not be given chance to vote. And it is not proper for any member of the club not to vote for the person he or she loves.
Please anybody not up to date should come forward in his or her gentility and pay their subscription before the D Day.

Management Committee

A boring little bird with a beak like a warped exclamation mark flipped about the upper reaches of a thorny tree, cheeping in some agitation at my presence in the shade below. Its nest wept like a hairy pear drop from a pliant stem, and in it were two light-grey eggs. Leaves had been bent down to keep off rain and sunshine. Many species of West African birds breed at the end of the rains when food is relatively abundant. I left the sun bird to its crib and strolled on through the greenery. My gym shoes hurt. I felt unfit and humid.

With Waz away I had moved about fifteen miles north from Gulak to Madagali where I spent a few days as the guest of a teacher. My memories were of a country eight years younger and newly reunified after civil war, of endless hills and silences, and, as I had swiftly realised, they were somewhat divorced from reality. The largest population of sub-Saharan Africa is shrugging off the Middle Ages, producing a tenth of the free world's oil annually and consuming colossal amounts of imported cement, steel and labour. I wondered how far off the roads and in what form the changes might have spread. I also wanted to break myself in with a few days' gentle strolling, and so I had wandered from Madagali into the hills which rose abruptly to the Cameroon border.

Scented pom-poms of the shrub *Acacia seyal* stood out like yellow lollipops among plots of guinea corn now eight and ten feet high and still a month from harvest. Worn by bicycles and undomesticated feet the path which I had taken dangled above the plain like an old dry vine, twisting up to the hill village of Visik between the boulders and the pale sterculia trees of the plateau edge. Giving vanity full reign I allowed a squall of hot frustration as I fiddled with the camera for a shot containing me, the path to Visik, and the rising plateau, but the damned thing kept falling over. I sat to cool down and along came fifteen tattered men from Mokolo, the nearest large town in the French speaking Cameroons. With a flurry of "Bonjour"s and "Merrrrci"s I arranged them in an old school pose and thrust the camera at the tallest. We smiled, he pressed the button, and must have shut his eyes. The result was a shot of bits of head and lots of sky, but I did not know it at the time. I was determined to bring back photos of Our Hero, a detail I had neglected on past trips. The labourers "au revoir, mon ami"-ed and padded on to Madagali for the next day's market.

Gasping like a whale on heat I stopped halfway up the hill and slumped across a rock. The path wound back across the quilted plain, the ripening patches not exactly fields but more like spheres of influence, shifting yearly, changing shape and size as families and obligations change, as fallow land is cleared again and old plots left in peace. My sense of order was disturbed by the casual arrangement spread below. How could

31

a land produce without the frozen marquetry of European field patterns?

To my foreign eyes the landscape lacked clear definition and at that moment symbolised the curtain of misapprehension and concealed assumptions that I, a European, bring to Africa.

A man called Moussa caught me up.

"Greetings, how's the road?" I said.

"There is road!" he said. "Where is tiredness and fatigue?"

"There is none," I said, lying through my teeth but following the prescribed ritual of Hausa greetings. "Welcome."

He took a head of sorghum (guinea corn) from his bag and rolling off the grain between his palms he offered me a trickle of green beads. The unripe seeds were rubbery and bits stuck in my teeth. More people passed us, bouncing down to Madagali market, each man with an empty plastic sack and strips of inner tube cut up to tie the load with which he would return to Cameroon.

We climbed on in silence to the top where Moussa took my cooking pot and vanished down a tree whose age and wisdom disappeared into the rocks. He stretched up on tiptoe from the hole and passed out the pot dripping brimful with a thickish purée through which, like soggy croûtons, cruised a fleet of rotting figs. The fruit had fallen off the tree. I drank as little as I could for according to the map Visik was close by and the going was reasonably flat.

We pushed on through the dangling corn like blinkered dwarfs. I saw the plateau rolling off in glimpses of far coloured hills, sweating shadowed bronze and gold into the ebbing sky. We must have walked another three miles before I questioned Moussa's leadership. He nipped back through the corn to a shelter we had seen, and shouted. A woman appeared. She had a large green shrub emerging from her navel. I made a mental note to inform the Royal Horticultural Society, then realised the shrub was purely decorative. She had another drooping down across her buttocks and a wooden sliver through her lower lip.

"Natives!" I thought, sitting down. Almost all Nigerians

have entered the broad Church of Islam or of Christianity and look with some embarrassment at ladies in the buff. According to prevailing thought, the past in Africa was generally bad and like a mob of puritans the Churches came to stamp it out. Islam has moved to standardise the north and the Christian Church has clothed the south. Both Churches seem to generate a joyless purity, the one in whose observance members make a grotesque imitation of some European prototype, the other in whose embrace a certain cultural dignity remains, despite the ritual straitjacket in which its adherents are so tightly laced.

The woman in leaves turned and called to a girl who stepped daintily across a ridged-up plot of sweet potatoes. She hitched her wrapper as she came, her nipples bouncing like a pair of dark sombreros, her gawky frame not quite at ease with the new inertias of pubescence. She sank down in respect at the presence of two men and listened as the woman told her to lead me back to Visik, which, submerged in corn, we had overshot. Moussa went off on his way and I followed the girl back across the fields until she stopped and pointed to a mud walled compound. Half a dozen men returned my greeting from their attitudes of rest beneath a mango tree. They had seen me wander by with Moussa. A boy brought water and a home-made deck chair into which I collapsed, sweat escaping quickly off my back, now rid of the unwelcome insulation of a ruck-sack.

A group of adults in Africa always seems to have a sort of asteroid belt of available children orbiting around it. A youthful missile was despatched to call the village teacher, obviously the only person a Bature would be interested in talking to. Bature is what Nigerians call Europeans. Meanwhile a ragged peasant appeared through the corn with a fresh and swelling bump upon his head. Somebody had smacked him with a hoe, but judging from the desultory grunts and casual streams of spittle leaving listless lips, the audience was not enormously impressed.

Suddenly my arm was seized and shaken violently. A dusty mass of wrinkled skin assembled in a ripped old pair of shorts and a jersey like a nest of disembowelled mice was lying down beside the deck chair. The old man lifted his jersey and pointed vigorously at a scab which clung like toast to his lower abdomen. Nursing something transistorised, the teacher arrived to explain that the man had fallen in a fire. The scab looked bulletproof. I poked around and found it dry with little inflammation but squirted it with cicatrin powder and gave the chap an aspirin which he treated like a holy wafer.

The teacher, though not fat, seemed despotically soft among the calloused bodies now dispersing to their compounds. He and the four other village teachers occupied two stone-walled huts and had some local women looking after them. They were on strike, because they had not received any pay for two months but in any case the village school had not yet been built and so the strike had little effect. Many prominent Africans, the President of Nigeria among them, have been primary school teachers at some stage in their lives but the primary teachers that I met were not a happy lot. For good or ill, English was the medium of instruction and many of the teachers knew less of it than the average parrot. They were the dross of the educational system which worked like a gigantic Catch 22, diverting those who failed to enter secondary school to the teacher training colleges and thence back to village schools as teachers. They were held in some respect by the peasantry, partly for their mumbo-jumbo but mostly because they theoretically received a regular salary. I thought of them as medieval village priests.

The headman pedalled up. He wore a thin white mackintosh and plastic shoes. His name was Usman and he had sore eyes. I put some drops in each and followed him inside the compound wall. We passed through the dissolving ruins of three old huts and came to the living quarters, built round a courtyard honed to naval cleanliness, freshly sanded and swept, and cool as an Asiatic garden. Usman had four women. One unrolled a mat against the wall of Usman's sleeping hut which had been cleared for my use, just as Garba in Kano had cleared his only bedroom.

The local fruit bats shook a leg from somewhere in the

mango trees and sent their Asdic chorus pinging out across the evening sky. Usman despatched a small boy off to get a lamp. Its impression grew inside the cap of darkness which had covered day with tropical formality, and within the enlarged shadows of its frame I taught Usman's sons to count completely up to ten and learn to say, "My eyes are brown and yours are green." We played with possessive pronouns and the brighter colours until my supper came, brought by Usman in blue enamel dishes on an enamel tray.

The boys dispersed. I was left in subtle privacy—physically surrounded, but with that space reserved in Africa in respect for guests who are taking food. I ate.

Licking tuwo off my hands I surprised myself with gestures I had picked up years before, when African food and eating without knives and forks had been something quite novel. Tuwo is the African equivalent of our daily bread. Made from the flour of guinea corn, millet, maize or rice, it is served with monotonous regularity from the Cape of Good Hope to the Sahara. Just as bread had become less of a staple in Europe, so, I imagine, will tuwo lose its stodgy monopoly in Africa, but only very very slowly. There are schemes afoot for Nigeria to grow large acreages of her own wheat, but tuwo remains a twice or three times daily fact of life over huge areas of Africa.

The first mosquitoes died that night of greedy curiosity in brownish smears along my arms and legs. There were fewer up here on the plateau than down below, but enough for me to wish I had a net. Domestic strife had broken out as I lay down to sleep. Usman and a woman were arguing in their own language, called Vomengu. It was something to do with where, or rather with whom, Usman would spend the night. Sweating damply in my sheet I thought of thistle down—the bed was awfully hard, a solid chunk of winterthorn (*Acacia albida*) about six feet long and two-and-a-half feet wide with stumpy six-inch legs, all hacked from a single piece.

Hornbills filled the morning sky like dodgems on the wing. The clumsy horde flew overhead with the scrappy incohesion of a stock-car race, honking at the rising sun. I was following my pupils of the night before, walking south across the stony bush to the hamlet of Mabas. They flicked odd chips of broken quartz up at the passing hornbills. I had gone into a toyshop before I left England to buy a small kaleidoscope, thinking it might be something nice to show to children on the way. I left the shop with the kaleidoscope as planned, but also with three Superballs, a set of jacks, a jigsaw and a catapult. With a leaping heart I had realised that technology had passed me by. The art of catapult design had transformed a boyhood symbol into quite a weapon, painted black, with arm rests and some amazing rubber which would not come off however hard you pulled.

Mabas was exquisitely constructed of the granite rock exposed in such profusion all around. The dry-stone compound walls were sheer and tight with heavy blocks for gate posts and foundations. A family in loincloths waved a greeting from a groundnut plot as the boys led me up into the shade of an enormous fig tree. A man in cotton robes appeared and greeted me in French. We had crossed the unmarked border and were in the Cameroons. The man thought I was from Mokolo and asked me where my car was.

The boys returned to Visik and after a revivifying brew I continued down the broken track which came from Mokolo. The plateau edge was less clearly defined now and actually rose towards the west in broken, convoluted hills. A gang of workmen patching up the road by hand directed me along a thin faint path which led back to Nigeria. A little valley grew as I went down between a maze of minute terraces picked out among the boulders, many supporting only half a dozen stalks of corn in the gravelly soil. House-sized boulders jumbled up the rugged hillside, echoing the shouts and piping cries of tribesmen scaring birds and rodents off the crops.

An isolated pinnacle hung above the main valley, a gigantic fang of rhyolite which had cooled and plugged the vent of a volcano, long since eroded, leaving the more resistant plug exposed. I was extremely hot and bothered, having lost the path and blundered into rough long grass that covered me in seeds and hay, but I could not resist the tooth of rock and, dumping off my rucksack, I worked my way up through the clinging vegetation. The actual climb was easy, but as I smoked a deserved cigarette I realised that I had lost my map. I tried to pick my route back down the Nggamachi valley to the flat ground south of Madagali and, although it looked a simple walk, I discovered that the undergrowth was so thick across the stream I had to crawl my way for several hours on my hands and knees, pulling my rucksack behind me. Eventually I reached a path, thoroughly disgruntled and discomfited.

A gurgling torrent flooded through the trees and over waggling grasses showing dimly green beneath the Marmite-coloured water. I had not suffered the pain of thirst for several years and had let the memory of total craving dim. I was not really thirsty now but felt the edge, when water needs a little time and shade to ease the dryness. However, I threw the stuff around like John the Baptist on a practice run and gradually smoothed the brackeny feeling in my mouth. I thought about my head and feet instead. My headache helped me to understand what eggs go through at hatching time and, at my other end, gym shoes abandoned, my tried and tested desert boots were bulging with the embarrassment of contents swollen in the heat. Having only walked about twenty-five miles my prospects for the forthcoming thousand did not seem very bright.

The stream dispersed down on the flatter ground among the compounds of the Vomengu, who had left the safety of the hills to make farms on the plains. I found the motor track from Madagali. It grew less formidably eroded and eventually started useful life beneath a tamarind in whose shade lolled several dozen drunks. I heard them from afar. A beer-up was in progress. The smell of children and diarrhoea rose with a peppered clump of flies and fumes within the beaten shade. Solid arms dispersed the flies, picked noses, hitched babies round to sleep and suck and dispensed calabashes of beer from red clay pots. The Vomengu women sat together, the older crones in leaves and leather, but the younger set in cotton wrappers with cracked half calabashes on their heads.

The men were sitting in the less dense shade and every few minutes one of them would stand up and shout very loudly at absolutely nothing. Others would gaze forlornly at an empty calabash then lurch over to the women, there to beg or buy more beer. Pairs would suddenly embrace, and, with mouths stuck side by side, drink down a bowl of beer together, a deft performance in the circumstances.

Four youths set off along the way that I had come, back up to Cameroon. They each had twenty-litre cans of petrol on their heads and several quarts of beer beneath their belts. My admiration was intense. I had taken no more than a sip at a crusty rim and hesitantly swallowed the fizzy gruel therein. It tasted of old yoghurt mixed with turps. A Datsun pick-up then arrived, reversed in gay oblivion among the staggering peasantry and roared off back to Madagali with me and several sacks of beans jostling from rut to rut at reckless speed.

All clean and fed that night I lay inside the courtyard of my hostess's house. The relief I felt at returning here to base was inconsistent with the lengthy plod I had in front of me—it was going to be a slog, especially in the humidity. At least the weather would be getting drier and cooler towards December.

4

The following day was not only a Saturday but it was the day of the Bornu State Schools Athletics Championships. The meeting was to be held in the afternoon at the Government secondary school, Bama, not fifty miles up the road. Waz was still away and I decided to attend.

By three o'clock the sports field had cooled sufficiently for the barefooted students to avoid cauterising themselves on the running track but they remained clustered sensibly in the shade. A bank of seats had been arranged beneath an awning into which the V.I.P.s gradually drifted. I sat down behind a sort of throne covered with red carpet and thick rugs and facing directly west. The guest of honour was going to roast. By three-thirty the sun's rays had slipped beneath the awning, warming up the silver cups arranged before the empty throne. The Shehu of Dikwa was late, and obviously no fool.

Meanwhile the sound of giant crisp bags giving birth erupted from the tannoy system. A teacher wrapped in flashy shades and spray-on strides leant forward to the microphone. His name was Ambrose. Two friends stood expressionless and silent at his side. I felt a twinge of exasperation—why are Africans always so frustratingly surrounded by hangers-on and relatives; why can't they get on with things on their own? Like Ambrose, about to give his speech, I was wearing glasses, a pair of European cultural filters.

It is precisely because Africans do not seem to exist as individuals in the way most Europeans might expect that strangers become so nonplussed in the rent-a-crowd African environment. An African is part and parcel of his social milieu and does not shed it readily: a man does not stand cut and dried alone, his edges and his margins fluctuate and merge with other presences which simply are because they are, requiring no special attention or excuse. If Europeans behave like drops of oil in water, Africans behave like drops of ink.

Ambrose began. His gracious introduction was, I felt, a little premature. Nevertheless he addressed the barren field and empty seats with some magnificence.

"Ladies and Gentlemen," he began quite unexceptionally, but then surprised us all with an enormous list which covered every conceivable state of human existence including teachers, visitors, Shehus, permanent secretaries, inspectors and ministers, possibly even angels and the hosts of heaven, none of whom had as yet turned up.

"Ladies and Gentlemen, de yong strong atleets, very yong and very strong are going to march past in wonderful colours." Pause. "They are getting ready now." Pause. "They are nearly ready." They obviously weren't. I could see confused milling from across the field as teachers tried to sort some kind of order for the parade.

"They're getting ready now, very pure and strong in fact, pure at least and uncontaminated yong."

A scattering of dignitaries caught the tail end of this teutonic raving, resplendent in their rigas, men of substance and great dignity, oblivious to the fact that absolutely nothing was going on. A fig tree blossomed with a flock of young spectators and the uncontaminated stream of youth moved slowly down the field. It picked up speed, urged on by the state inspector of schools, a short fat Yoruba in tight white shorts and a woollen shirt. Faster and faster ran the yong strong atleets, swallowing the fat inspector whole. They swept him forward, round the running track, his whistle screeching faintly out across the sand, then someone tripped and whirlpools of confusion spun within the prancing torrent.

From sources deep inside the dusty shambles came the fat inspector, looking like a knackered mole and blowing hard. Order was eventually restored and Ambrose announced the first events, actually the long jump and the high jump. There seemed to be a muddle as to which was which despite a multitude of referees festooned with measuring tapes, time-pieces and spare whistles. There was even one old hand within the crowd, an Englishman with thirty years' experience of teaching in the tropics, sporting a pair of brass binoculars, a white felt hat and blazer, and a shooting stick. He brought back poignant memories of unenthusiastic knees in drizzle on the playing fields of somewhere totally irrelevant to the town of Bama in Nigeria.

Ambrose's loud appeals for competitors bore fruit in the form of an orange bobble cap containing one small and knobbly boy who hurled himself along the runway to the long jump pit, but in the wrong direction, landing in a painful spray of thorny shrub and bobble. His brave but useless effort did at least stir up some spirit in the crowd and other athletes took the field. Things were hurled and flung spasmodically, but the real drama of the afternoon came with the sprinting.

The fat inspector officiated at the start line with a pair of sawn off .303s, five cartridges to each magazine. He waved the shortened rifles round his head with the firmness of a palsied firing squad. The ammunition was, of course, very much alive. The timekeeper, I noted from the programme, was called Mr. Pannicker. I ducked as a hail of fire called back the finalists in the hundred-yard dash who had made a shaky start, amazed that half of them weren't winged or dead. I wondered if the Nigerian Olympic team trained in body armour. The sprinters took off the second time like bats out of hell, shot past the finishing post and disappeared into the distant cover of the school buildings.

The last event, to quote the programme, was the "Short Pot". My visions of a host of debagged students streaking through the bush with the fat inspector firing wildly behind them were interrupted by the "Vot of Thanks" proposed by Ambrose. I missed the presentation of the silver cups shimmering in pride of place before the still vacant chair of honour. I hope the Shehu when he came was warned and didn't burn his hands.

41

5

Days in Gulak went by on trays of rice and meat cooked for us by Waziri's aunts. We lived in bachelor quarters within the compound of the district head who was away in Mecca. Within the high outer wall of mud grew fronds of sorrel, mango trees and paw paw plants. Pumpkins lay in pregnant solitude along green vines half hidden in the grass where cats caught mice and chickens scuffed for chaff spilled from wooden mortars. The sounds of women pounding grain, of children laughing at the moon and throbbing diesels grinding corn were part of the daily round. Waz had his social obligations and I had to be patient. I had agreed to delay our departure until the public festival was over, but I grew hot and listless waiting. One evening I went for a walk on the rocky slopes behind the village.

The ragged edges of a vulture's wing, immensely high, were carding wisps of storm cloud from the west. The bird was turning slowly on the livid yellow banks, a tiny spider dangling in the vastness of the thunder. A soft, white gust of wind shot the angled shadow of a hawk across the hill, a billowing towel of air which hardened tight against the drying leaves and zauna mats in the village down below. The sun went down in smoky virulence and bush fires twinkled on the plain. The wind began to howl and then it rained. It rained like refugees, it rained unstoppably, unthinkingly, like demons on cocaine. And then, quite suddenly, it stopped. It was the last rain of the season.

The dampness evaporated rapidly and within twenty-four hours I was lying with my back against a tree, watching the toads skipping across the main square of Gulak. The moonlight shone brightly off their backs and off their shocked black eyes. The tale of Abraham was being broadcast by a group of preachers called the Friends of Islam, but my Hausa was only good enough to catch the odd word. I left the crowded square and walked away towards the sound of drumming coming from the area of the village where the Matakams lived in their small conical huts. They came from the nearby hills and were less influenced by the evangelists than the "down people" as the plains dwellers were called. The Matakams did the menial jobs around Gulak, labouring in the fields and sending the money back to their relatives across the border.

A group of lads was standing in the light of a bonfire, whopping an enormous drum, while others blew their lungs out down the horns of cows. The dancers, mostly women, did subtle things to the monotonous beat. They all carried green branches. Appropriate quantities of beer were being drunk. I had some and felt ill. In the small hours I got up to make myself sick. I was producing enough gas to fill a barrage balloon and felt like a bombed out sewage farm. The dance had actually been part of a funeral rite: "The Waltz of the Living Dead," I thought, but I recovered my morale by midday and refuelled that night in Gwoza where I had been invited to a thanksgiving party given by Canadian friends. I met a couple there who invited me to spend the weekend at their home in Biu, about five hours' drive away.

The villages that we passed through were throbbing, full and crowded for the holiday. The roads were fairly dangerous. We reached Biu and began to drive through the town. I noticed two things. The first was a blue notice with red lettering. "Leadway Insurance", it said. "Built on a rocky foundation." The second thing was a child, running through the dappled shade then off the swirling roadside. I think that his mind had already flown across the street, but his body dithered, did not see, and ran again, colliding with that split second of eternity when, since there is nothing you can do, your "you"ness disappears. It comes back pretty fast, though, smacks you right in the guts with a sandbag of adrenalin. We scrunched to a halt with smoking tyres and burst out of the car.

He wasn't there.

Oh God! Scrabbling hands and backs all heaving up the running-board, he's, Jesus, yes, oh Christ, I pulled him out, a sick sweet smell all warm and broken like a rodent under claws. Mouth full of little bits, open up, thank Christ, it's chewed up sugar cane and not his teeth. Not bleeding much— a hospital. Stop a car. Jump in with the bundle in my shirt, it's only half a mile and leave him on the couch at Casualty. Go off to report to the police.

Graham, who had been driving, and I walked up the steps into the police station. An extremely tough looking sergeant was coming down the stairs, all boots and starch. We began to explain what had happened. The sergeant did not seem to be listening.

"What is this man?" he said.

"What?" we said.

"This Nigeria Police. What is this man? You cannot come to Nigeria Police improperly dressed. This man should put his sirt." My shirt was at the hospital. The sergeant was angry. Paranoid wog. I nearly blew it. Graham pacified him and I asked if I could wash the blood off my arms. We made statements and all became sweetness and light. There had already been eleven accidents in Biu that day.

We returned to the hospital, saw the doctor, commiserated with the boy's family, brought piles of fruit and orange squash for him and went home. The child's right femur was broken and he was still unconscious but so far there were no signs of internal injuries or brain damage.

We spent a blank evening with sandwiches and some rather welcome Mozart which iced the shade of Graham's house. It was nice inside the capsules run by Europeans where the outer world impinged only via houseboys, power cuts and bone dry plumbing. However, it was definitely time to start and, having returned to Gulak for one more night, we did.

44

6

A pylon and the wind vanes which once pumped water for the
village of Gulak lay behind our compound, overgrown and
roosted on by chickens. Local sales of leather well buckets,
"gugas" as they were called, had revived greatly with this
technological reversal, as had sales of "rope". I use this term
loosely. So did the drawers of water. Bowlines and clove-
hitches were not their strong points. The problems of loose
knots and frayed rope were compounded by the varying and
uncertain distances from the well heads down to the water
level, which tended to drop spasmodically from October onwards. This variable factor presents an interesting challenge
to the thinking man upon a Gulak morning, a challenge nobly
ignored by one and all. The tendency was for these latter day
Jebusites to trust in the Lord, chucking their gugas down the
wells without, as the local V.D. clinic might say, Taking
Adequate Precautions. Adequate Precautions in this case included tying the free end of the rope to a fixed object, but the
people of Gulak tended to ignore such petty details in the heat
of the moment, the result being a dawn chorus of loud splashes
and exclamations of "Allah!", which roughly translated means
"Fuck!"

On the morning of our departure, gugas must have
plummeted down the wells like depressed lemmings. It took
Dan Asabe, our man about the village, an hour to find one.
We wanted a wash and some tea before we left for Baga. We
also wanted to leave early because travelling in the heat of
the day was unpleasant. So was what Dan Asabe eventually
pulled up from the depths—a gugaful of greenish fluid with

a suspension of mud, feathers and bird shit. A duck had fallen down the well.

The great trek was delayed but we eventually shouldered our packs (a sobering experience) and walked down to the main road with wishes of good luck from all and sundry as we passed. We bought a few supplies in Maiduguri where we had to wait through the midday heat at the Baga road lorry park. I sat in the shade of a truck which was the motor industry's answer to the Hunchback of Notre Dame. The chassis was so twisted that, head on, you could see all three wheels quite clearly. The fourth was missing. West African trucks never really die, but, adapting to the changing realities of old age and oncoming traffic, they simply carry different things. The very oldest seem to retire into the firewood business, doddering along on local journeys with plenty of off-the-piste stuff and not too much time spent on proper roads. My truck had brought a load of yams up from the south. Yam and sugar-cane transport was a little further upmarket than firewood which could always be abandoned in emergency without financial ruin. A human chain, which I declined to join, was unloading and stacking the yams into ordered piles protected from the withering sun by a layer of straw. Other than that not much was going on. The sense of impending desolation was quite strong. We were heading north towards the driest part of Nigeria where, at our start point, the annual rainfall is less than ten inches and daytime temperatures of 115°F are quite normal. It was about the last place you would expect to find a lake.

Among many strange facts about Lake Chad is the news that the water is fresh. Most desert lakes are saline. Lake Disappointment in Australia is a good example. With evaporation exceeding precipitation by a factor of about ten, one might expect at least the northern part of the lake to be a sort of Dead Sea, but in fact Lake Chad is one of the world's richest sources of wild freshwater fish. The waters of the lake disappear under the northern shore, seeping beneath the Sahara desert where they eventually come to a halt and dry up, leaving the precipitated salts miles away from the open water. It is also thought that the rather specialised lacustrine vegetation deals with the salts in some way. It struck me that a rather good Ph.D. project was going to waste.

Another local feature of note was the Baga road, perhaps better suited to the attentions of a chain gang than of an academic. Man-on-Wheels against Nature is a standard opening gambit for travel books on Africa. The Baga road was a stretch of Man-on-Wheels against Man. It was built in the mid 1960s to link Baga, then a major lake port, and Maiduguri, and it greatly facilitated the transport of dried fish to the important markets of the south. After fifteen years' hard use it facilitated very little. The only beneficiaries of what had become a 126-mile-long obstacle course were the flies and a species of beetle which specialises in eating dead fish. The flies and the beetles took full advantage of the increasing journey time by munching their way through the slow moving cargoes aboard the lorries jolting south. The Baga road was like a stage set for the First World War. Vehicles would actually get stuck in the tarmac which was in places heaped and rutted like deep mud. Some stretches of the road were raised on causeways across parts of the country liable to flood. These were the exciting bits where lorries would sway towards each other, weaving between the potholes with their axles doing yoga. Occasionally we passed the burnt-out shell of a car nestling in a crater, and once we looked down on the extraordinary spectacle of two donkeys making love, at which Waz and I broke into a rendering of the Beatles' number, "Why don't we do it in the road?"

Blues and dark rich purples lined the western sky, an even course of cool deep colour dissipating the accumulated lethargy of too much heat. The market place near Gajiram where we had stopped for evening prayers was almost abandoned. Six horsemen rode away into the open bush, their spears evocative of war and deeds done long ago. Waz went off to get some water. The moon hung in the east and flames from a crackling grass fire accentuated the gathering night. The bush is burnt off deliberately and as soon as possible around the northern villages to prevent fire sweeping through them later as the dry season advances.

"I had to pay," Waz said, handing me our plastic bottle.

"What for?" I asked.

"The water, they asked me for some money." We were moving quickly up towards the desert fringe.

We plodded through the moonlight and into the compound of the Chad Basin Development Authority, just a mile short of Baga. I had met one of the expatriates who worked there and had been invited to stay. In addition to its exotic vegetation and complying with its swampy nature, the lake supports a writhing bureaucracy of Agencies, Commissions, Authorities, Organisations and Institutes, all strictly regulated according to the $E=mc^2$ of human nature, Parkinson's Law. Despite its impressive scenery, the world of the international civil service is actually rather similar to that of the local town hall with its intractable problems of disappearing teaspoons and a decent choice of biscuits at elevenses.

Our host was a bearded Cornish man who had been in Baga for nearly two years. Tim was interested in our plan to climb Mount Cameroon, having run hapless youths up and down its thirteen-thousand-foot slopes as an instructor at an Outward Bound school that the colonial administration used to run at Man o' War Bay. He now worked for the Food and Agricultural Organisation which lives in Rome. He ran a small boatshed where people were building flat bottomed canoes for use on the lake. We were taken to his house by a neat Indian gentleman who had crammed us into his Volkswagen beetle. My rucksack frame became tangled in his wife's sari as we got out.

Tim had all that a man could want—electricity, music, air conditioning and eggs. His wife was back in England settling their children into school but he had a chap out from the Tropical Products Institute staying with him who spent his time sniffing round the Baga fish market in a rather inhibited way. He had come to check on the losses caused by the dermestid beetle, one of those pieces of "research" which any Boy Scout could knock off in five minutes flat. He was a clean bush hat and shorts sort of bloke who did not shake hands with Waz, an omission due, I think, to confusion. He had, after all, been trained to handle infested fish, not people, and in any case Waz had buried himself in a comic, either *Newsweek* or *Time*, which did little to assist the smooth flow of social intercourse.

In the morning Tim showed us round. Money had been spent on a colossal scale in two general directions. To the north-west lay the Polder, a carefully ruled embankment of earth about eight feet high and fifteen feet across. Holding the earth in place was a continuous wall of iron shuttering, pile-driven into the dry lake bed.

"There's thirty-six kilometres of it," Tim said. My mouth fell open. Every one of the hundred thousand iron pilings used in its construction had been carted up from Lagos and at about four to the ton I could see that it was not only the passage of smoked fish that had contributed to the donkeys' love nest on the Baga road. The Polder was intended to be an artificial shore line, protecting the land behind it from inundation when the lake rose. Irrigated with lake water, the protected land was to become a vast prairie of nodding wheat, which, as Tim drily pointed out, was an expensive way of making sandwiches. Home produced wheat would, however, reduce an increasingly large import bill and satisfy the nation's rapidly developing taste for bread and cakes. There was, unfortunately, a slight hitch. The lake had vanished. Maddening. To rectify this problem money had been despatched to the north-east, scudding through the bush in the form of a canal, to date twenty-seven kilometres long, and, or have you guessed, roughly eight feet deep and fifteen feet wide.

The canal ended in a pool just behind Tim's house. A dredger was moored on the pool and as we walked by a straw hat scuttled ashore. Strange to say, it spoke Greek. Somewhere inside it was the captain of the dredger, a dwarfed Hellene who also knew some English. He had been with the dredger for fifteen years. It came to bits and could, he said, be assembled anywhere. At the moment work had stopped due to hostile native action. The dredger, cutting through the more or less useless swamp, had revived enormous interest in local history. People were finding that their fathers and grandfathers had been using the land since time immemorial and were putting in amazing claims for compensation to the local authority. There had been a bit of spear waving and the odd arrow had been seen flying in the direction of the weird machine as it ploughed forward, pursuing the receding waters ever further into the Sahara, and it had been decided to stop digging in case someone got hurt.

The canal would eventually bring water from the lake to the areas earmarked for wheat production, in principle an excellent scheme. The old lake bed is, despite its sandy appearance, very fertile. The first European in the area, a man called Dixon Denham, had remarked in 1823 that "if the land were cleared of wood almost anything might be grown". He also noticed how far the water could encroach in a single day. Being very shallow in relation to its surface area, variations in the volume of lake water have drastic consequences, leaving thousands of square miles either dry as a bone or six feet under. Heinrich Barth, a German who followed up Denham's discoveries, was also impressed by the lake's volatile nature. Having spent a fruitless Thursday in 1851 straining his eyes to see it, he concluded that it was "an immense lagoon, changing its border every month and therefore incapable of being mapped with accuracy".

Nine-tenths of the lake arrives from the south, discharged by the River Chari which drains land hundreds of miles away in the Central African Republic. The timing of this annual flood is predictable. The lake has usually spread furthest by February and has shrunk to a minimum in July. Unfortunately the extent of inundation is highly variable, which is why the Polder was not a likely candidate for the Dutch thumb treatment, and also why the Greek was extending his contract—a man who was, in every sense, opening up a continent and presumably dredging his way into the *Guinness Book of Records*.

That night we had dinner with Dr. J. E. Moess, an amiable character, but not liked by everybody. He was the head of the local section of the Development Authority and theoretically Tim's boss. He obviously knew the F.A.O. ropes backwards and according to local rumour he was about to find the rigging come tumbling about his ears. He was about sixty years old, nearly bald, with an arched little nose, a clipped beard, and an enormous stomach. His navel winked enthusiastically from his gay cotton shirt and he sat with the steadfastness of a buddha on a jolly good bush allowance. Dr. Moess had been born in Surinam, and being of Dutch extraction had acquired a Dutch wife who remained in obscurity in Holland. His present companion was a large Tanzanian lady called Mary.

In Moess was represented a subtle blend of Africa and Europe. His academic reputation, so he told me, rested upon honours bestowed by an American university for his consideration of the role of local finance in industrial projects. He did not bore us with the details but kicked off with an entertaining description of the use to which he put his research and development fund. His name for it was The Research and Entertainment Fund. He was not a man who took his pleasures lightly. Old Moess had things figured out in a realistic way. No pappy idealism for him. He thought the Polder project was a complete white elephant, but as he said, "Der Echipshuns pild der Pryamits, der Pridish pild der Concort, vy not der Nicheerans dey pild der Polter?" I wanted to know about the bush but he insisted on talking about Lagos, which he loved. He is the only human being who I have ever heard expressing less than loathing for that city. I finally got him on to the right track.

"I vent inder boosh vonce." His eyes glazed. After a prolonged silence he brightened and looked up. That, apparently, was that. "Haf you zeen der refews of my book?" he asked. The boosh was not of great interest. We left Baga the following morning.

51

7

Conditions aboard the white pick-up to which we had committed ourselves for the sixty-mile journey north from Baga
to Mallam Fatori were uncomfortable. Within a very few
leagues I had acquired the mental outlook of a pilchard, being
both squashed and cooked, but at least the ever thinning bush
was flat.

The vegetation was typical of the sahel (literally "the shore"
in Arabic), a transition zone between the desert proper and the
savannahs. Large areas had already been burnt off and were
bare of the knee high straw and the tangled thorn that otherwise
covered the sand. Some sections of the track had been cut
straight through the thorn breaks and we churned along for
spindly miles, stopping occasionally to retrieve turbans and
shawls which had been caught in the branches.

We decanted ourselves at a village about halfway through
the day, plonking down to wait in the shade of a neem tree
while our vehicle went off on some local errand. It was far
too hot for Meaningful Conversation but a fellow passenger
engaged us with a brief display of his war wound. His name
was William and he had been hit in the abdomen by a piece of
shrapnel during the Nigerian Civil War twelve years earlier.
He was still in the army and was on his way to rejoin his unit
on frontier duty near Mallam Fatori, which actually used to
be on the lake shore. It was the lake which had moved, not
the town.

Lake Chad is a cosmopolitan sort of a puddle, not much
more than ten feet deep, and not really sure of its true
nationality. Both Nigeria and the Francophone republics of

Chad, the Cameroons and Niger have slices of it on their books, but the water shifts about rather unpatriotically. The whole area receives a good deal of military attention. The Nigerians even have a few of those marsh skippers associated with a well known brand of intoxicant, but when I arrived they had broken down, having run out of ice and lemon I presumed.

Over on the eastern shore the republic of Chad was still in the throes of a civil war which had dragged on for years. Chad is the poorest and most isolated country in Africa, two-thirds desert and the rest hungry. The war had made headlines in the West only when the occasional anthropologist had been held to ransom, but had recently increased in news value with the arrival of the Libyans who had rudely gate-crashed from the north. Three days before we arrived in Baga an event had occurred unsurpassed for excitement since Nigeria changed to driving on the right. A Libyan helicopter had landed in the bush and our friend Tim had rushed out to see it. The eight-man crew, immaculate in white shorts and socks, were to be seen for some days as guests of the soldiers quartered behind Tim's compound. They were eventually flown down to Lagos and handed back to Libya. They had been en route for Chad with a cargo of guns, rockets and, strangely, whips.

William, of the abdominal war wound, had retained the rank of private soldier throughout his fifteen years' service, but at least he had been on the winning side in the Nigerian Civil War. Ernest, a native of Onitsha also propping up our neem tree, had not. He was an Ibo, and he dealt in soft drinks. He was touring the scrub, drumming up business, which is the sort of thing that Ibos do. The wilds of Africa are very strange nowadays. Instead of ostrich and gazelle, the "sahel" is alive with men in pick-up trucks discussing war and fizzy orange juice. Ernest, too, was very much a foreigner in Bornu. He was several shades darker than the locals who, he said, were like people in "the movings". The swords, bows and spears of the gowned Fulani herdsmen who had been sharing the back of the pick-up with us did lend a certain cinematic drama to the scene.

"Dis Fulani, dey got plenty cash," said Ernest, "One cow cost four hundred naira and dey so many de boos be full. Why dey kip dis cows but no fit buy Peugeot?" Maybe Waz and I would find out once we had started walking. We were looking forward to encountering the nomadic Fulani and Shuwa Arab herdsmen on their own terms.

Between Mallam Fatori and the Mediterranean coast lie fifteen hundred miles of nothing very much. As a last outpost of civilisation the town was pretty dull except for a jeep-load of prostitutes cruising about the sandy streets in low ratio. They were from Bosso, just across the Yobe river in the French speaking republic of Niger. Before the establishment of European rule the whole area had been part of the empire of Kanem-Bornu, at the southern end of what used to be a major caravan route leading north over the Sahara to Tripoli. Small as it is, the Yobe is the first open river in roughly twenty degrees of latitude and must have been a welcome sight for both merchants and soldiers coming out of the desert.

Dixon Denham, Captain 3rd Regiment of Foot, and Major, "Continent of Africa only", was the first European to cross the desert to Bornu and return alive. He reached the Yobe from Tripoli on 4 February 1823. The populace, ". . . flying acrofs the plain in all directions . . ." was eventually calmed and Denham brought some essential supplies, ". . . a lamb for two bits of amber . . . two needles purchased a fowl, and a handful of salt four or five good sized fish from the lake."

"The great lake," wrote Denham, "glowing with the golden rays of the sun in its strength, appeared to be within a mile of the spot on which we stood . . ." On roughly that same spot, in the year of our Lord nineteen hundred and eighty, the only thing glowing was me, with heat. The great lake was nowhere in sight. All I could see, apart from the receding prostitutes, were heaps of ruined Land-Rovers. The town of Mallam Fatori appeared to have been built in a scrapyard and the inhabitants were either asleep in the shade or mining spare parts out in the sun.

Denham's expedition succeeded because the Bashaw of Tripoli, who was matey with the English, provided a full time escort of two hundred mounted tribesmen. He also had a number of important Bornuese hostages secreted at an oasis in what is now central Libya. The Earl Bathurst, His Majesty's Principal Secretary of State for the Colonies, had given Denham careful instructions. He was requested to "explore the country to the southward and eastward of Bornu, principally with a view of tracing the course of the Niger, and ascertaining its embouchure . . ." Central Africa was still a land of utter darkness. The prevailing wisdom had it that the Niger flowed into the Nile, with randy gorillas patrolling the banks and natives sporting tails or worse. In the four hundred years since the Portuguese had gone down beyond Cap Bojador in their caravels, tacking southward on lateen sails and with new fangled sternpost rudders, no European had got further inland than the steaming deltas of a few major rivers. South America, by contrast, had been swarming with conquistadors within a few years of discovery. Part of the reason was medical. Even in the 1890s the geologist Mr. Harold Bindloss could write of the Nigerian coast that,

> . . . the pestilence is always there, and when forest and swamp are rolled in a fever mist at the change of seasons men die one after another or suffer in burning torment. The inhabitants are cannibals, devil-worshippers and offerers of human sacrifices . . . it is a land where murdered slaves drift down the muddy creeks.

Denham and his companions had seen their share of dead slaves, too, victims of the brutal march north to the markets of Tripoli. On the eve of Christmas, 1822, Denham records passing "an average of sixty to eighty or ninety skeletons a day; but the numbers that lay around the wells at El Hamer were countless." The eventual suppression of the slave trade was the distant hope of many early explorers of Africa.

The Earl Bathurst's original instructions to the expedition of 1822 are preserved in the Public Records Office. A series of curt little notes between Denham and Hugh Clapperton, the expedition's navigator, is also kept there. Relations between the two men were strained from the first. I wondered if Waz and I would be reduced to communicating with each other in ink. "I had hoped," writes Denham (the letter is headed "Tents"), "that a mutual disposition to amiable cooperation would have made our journey of discovery with all its necefsary disagreeables at least one of harmony but that unfortunately appears impofsible . . ."

It looked like an old interservice rivalry. Clappers was a naval type, thirty-four years old, "handsome, athletic and powerful", according to his brother. He went to sea in the merchant fleet at thirteen, had been impressed into the Royal Navy and was subsequently wounded and shipwrecked. Having commanded a blockhouse against the French in Canada he was not amenable to being ordered about by a major, albeit "Continent of Africa only". Here is an extract from Clapperton's reply, also written from "Tents" and dated 1 January 1823. ". . . you [Denham] take upon yourself a great deal to issue such orders which could not be more imperative were they from the Horse Guards or the admiralty. You must not introduce a martial system into what is civil and scientific . . ." I imagine that the third member of the expedition, Walter Oudney, M.D., spent his time floundering across the dunes, perhaps kicking aside the odd skull, to deliver these stupid notes.

The cruising prostitutes again hove to during our first evening in town. We were strolling in from the state fisheries compound where we had established ourselves. Our letter of introduction from headquarters in Maiduguri had been almost unnecessary as the chap in charge had welcomed us profusely. Mr. Bitrus was, in fact, a rather lonely man. He came from a predominantly Christian area in the far south of the state, and although he had spent five years up here in Kanuri territory he did not speak the language. On hearing of our plan to follow the lake shore he immediately expressed a wish to join us. His duties, light as they were, prevented him from coming along but he was thoroughly fed up with the boredom of being a fisheries officer with no fish to look after. The lake had vanished years ago and the research station had been left high and dry.

The abandoned bungalow which Mr. Bitrus had made available for our use was studied with inert piles of *The Fishing Gazette*. The earliest copies went back to 1958 and were almost archaeological finds. The knobbly kneed spirits of colonial boffins billowed out from the dusty pages, innocent of nylon fishing line, sociology and decent colour printing. Twenty years earlier the compound had basked on the lake shore with open water stretching to the horizon. It must have been an idyllic posting, but things had changed drastically. A few overgrown canoes lay in the nearby scrub and further out in the bush the improbable hulk of a twenty foot cruiser lurked among the trees. Despite the departure of the lake both state and federal authorities maintained research establishments in the area. I wondered why. Most of the fish I saw in Mallam Fatori had been caught by the wily Iberians and the Japanese and had been exported to Nigeria in tins. Oil money is strange stuff. I had read in *The New Nigerian* newspaper an advertisement inviting tenders for the construction of cold storage plants all over the north. The plants were to cater for the planned importation of thousands of tons of fresh mackerel from northern Europe. In the same paper was another invitation to tender, this time to the Nigerian Pilgrims Board, for the contract to supply seventy thousand suitcases and matching travellers' bags in different colours "in order to assist the pilgrims in identifying their luggage". Oil from the Christian south of the country has enabled tens of thousands of Muslims from the Islamic north to perform at least once in their lives the sacred duty of pilgrimage to Mecca.

We were supplied, in our bungalow, with the surprising luxury of fresh running water. It was piped under natural pressure from a nearby borehole. A little patch of lime trees and mangoes shaded the well head in luscious contrast to the surrounding desiccation. On the way up from Maiduguri we had seen several roadside waterholes created by a drilling programme which has tapped the fresh water aquifers underlying the Chad Basin. Unfortunately many of the wells are uncapped and water gushes forth into stagnant ponds where stock, people, and all manner of slime combine in diseased content.

The Chad drainage basin covers about half a million square miles but the size of the actual lake has varied enormously. About fifty thousand years ago it covered an area twice the size of France, although it is also known to have dried up completely just before the last Ice Age. In the early sixties the lake covered about nine thousand square miles. It has now shrunk to less than a quarter of that size. A barrier of windblown vegetation and sand has formed right across it just to the north of Baga, causing an interesting hiccup in the annual rise and fall of the lake level. The barrier has created two separate pools, and it is only when the southern pool is full that the water can spill over into the northern section. As a consequence the northern pool does not usually fill up until February and, unfortunately for us, it had actually failed to rise at all in recent years and was now almost completely dry.

It had been a relief to have found so congenial a base from which to look for local guides. We needed someone to help us along the first stage of our journey. From our planned start point in Mallam Fatori the idea had been to walk out to the lake shore and south in the direction of Baga, but it was something of a disappointment to discover that the lake had receded so drastically that there was in fact no shore to follow. We still needed a guide, though. The maps which I had bought in Maiduguri were based on aerial photographs taken at the time of the Korean War and were virtually useless. We had decided to strike out across the dry lake bed and head for Baga by the most direct route rather than tamely follow the sandy ruts of the jeep track which had brought us to Mallam Fatori, but we did not know the way.

Mr. Bitrus promised to spread the word around the adjacent Kanuri settlements and assured us that we would find our guides. Meanwhile we took him for a drink. A dozen minibuses were laagered near the town centre, gleaming in the moonlight. A rally of the Greater Nigeria People's Party was to be held the following day and the ladies in the jeep had stopped to ask us where the pre-rally action was. They anticipated business and were dressed accordingly. I nearly decided to go into politics. It had been a tiring day and, according to Dixon Denham, "A little oil or fat from the hand of a negress (all of whom are taught the art of shampooing to perfection) rubbed well round the neck and loins and back is the best cure." This sounds like a reasonable conclusion to a hard day at the office, but I am not sure if "shampooing" is the word for it. Despite possible misgivings the major, "Continent of Africa only", appears to have winked and thought of England at least once or twice because although, "from my Christian belief I was deprived of possessing half a dozen of these shampooing beauties . . . the wife of my negro . . . Zerega . . . was the greatest use to me on these occasions of fatigue . . ." My own Christian belief is fairly keen on a good rub down but what held me back was the likely price. Nigeria is an expensive country and inflation is rampant. I made do with a nourishing Maltex instead. This is a non-alcoholic beverage which tastes like equal parts of Guinness and fermented gravy. For the most nauseating effects it should be drunk at Mallam Fatori room temperature which averages out at a bracing 98.4°. That night I had a vivid dream about hairdressers.

I was twenty-two when I had my first close encounter with a Nigerian lady. I had given her a lift on the back of my motorbike and nearly fell off with excitement in the first hundred yards. The poor girl had to hang on to something, but it became increasingly obvious, even in my then state of sexual curacy, that she had a marked preference for some handholds over others. Swerving on in reluctant ecstasy I was fondled like a scrap of pornographic braille for another six miles. The journey was a nightmare.

I had recently been working in a remote area of bush for the Wildlife Preservation Unit then based in Jos and had returned to prepare my report, leaving behind a game guard called Ishaya whose mind worked with the approximate speed of cold toffee. He was very, very thick but he had a fierce regard for his family and I had promised to check that his wife properly received her allowances in his absence. Although I had never met her I had arranged to pick her up, and kept a sharp lookout. When I saw a feminine wave from the agreed road junction I had stopped and a very sexy lady clambered aboard without question. I naturally assumed that the hands so swiftly down my trousers were those of my game guard's wife. "Just the sort of woman poor old Ishaya would have," I thought, panting faintly. With her nipples boring into my shoulder blades we swept up to the office, a palatial reminder of the days when Jos produced a good proportion of the world's tin and consumed gin on a like scale. The building had been slung up in the acme of bad taste, a cross between Anne Hathaway's cottage and the Castle Douglas.

Unbalanced by the morning's laying on of hands, I paused in the hallway to recover my equanimity and to check my flies. I then escorted my willowy passenger to the boss's office. At that time the chief wildlife officer was an Englishwoman and a leading expert on the African elephant, an animal which she paid the great compliment of imitating. Most people called her "Sir". Feudal with "natives", imperial with her gun, and Victorian with money, she was a strange blend and not easy to work for. Today she was being feudal.

"Here's Ishaya's wife," I said. "Oh yes," she replied, giving my masseuse a hypocritical beam, "how nice to see you again, dear." I translated and she chatted on, giving me the impression that she knew her staff and their families creditably well. I assumed that the two women had met several times before but got a rather blank reaction to my translation. I put this down to my imperfect Hausa, but "dear" seemed to grasp the financial side of things and was asked to wait while the necessary payment vouchers were prepared. A considerable sum was then handed to her, but instead of leaving she stayed. I had by this time gone for a long overdue pee. Imagine my surprise, and my consequently wild marksmanship, when she walked in and sat on the bath. She had obviously never seen a white one before and that went for the bath too. My knees threw instant wobblers and it took somewhat longer than usual to adjust my dress. I was acutely embarrassed and made frenzied attempts to keep her on the bath. Ishaya was bound to find out. "Oh Jesus," I thought, desperately worried in case somebody appeared. Jesus did not help. I wondered how the Vatican dealt with nymphomaniacs.

Half expecting a delegation from the *News of the World*, I emerged from the loo and, creeping across the hall like a spotlit flasher, I staggered into my office. The extremely attractive voyeur was not long behind me, loosening her wrapper as she came in. Did Ishaya know of his wife's interests, I wondered, as she draped a thigh over the desk? I tried to concentrate on my report but it was impossible. My dress was again slowly unadjusted and as my eyesight became increasingly blurred it gradually dawned on me that I had MADE A GHASTLY MISTAKE.

I had thought that my boss knew Ishaya's wife. My boss had thought that I knew Ishaya's wife. What Ishaya's wife thought no one would ever know because the lady down my trousers whose hands had been roaming definitely wasn't her. After a lengthy interview she turned out to be a prostitute who had been on her way to the local barracks and had simply given me a friendly wave. She was used to being picked up by strange men, but considered the European's custom of getting his "mother" to pay for services rendered a little unusual.

Taking her back to the road junction was rather less of a thrill than our earlier journey. As I drove away I fancied that I could hear mocking laughter from other, equally attractive women also stationed at the corner, and also waiting for nice gentlemen to take them for a drive. Ishaya had chosen the naughtiest rendezvous in town and on my few remaining mornings in Jos I accelerated past it in what I hoped would appear an indistinguishable blur.

The political rally was in full swing when we returned to the town the following day. Dancers and drummers were performing for a large crowd outside the house of the district headman. After thirteen years of military rule, civilian government had recently broken out and politics had again taken its rightful place as the national sport. Having been through a terrible civil war, Nigerians are acutely conscious of the need to create one nation in a land of extreme cultural diversity. The formation of new political parties had been so dominated by a concern to avoid charges of ethnic particularism that ideological considerations assumed a relatively minor significance. The division of the country into nineteen states had produced a fluid state of political power which the elections of the previous year had not entirely settled. The "political process" was being pursued with characteristically African exuberance all over the country. The rally at Mallam Fatori remained peaceful although as we turned to go a dazed young man was led away, blood rolling down his face and splattering his cotton robe. We did not discover if he had been hit or just run over in the excitement.

I had once been privileged to live through a general election campaign in Colombia, a display of Brylcreemed histrionics which had left the whole country thoroughly plastered. There had been posters everywhere. The Andean sun had filtered but weakly through windows obscured with mug shots of the local politicos, turning the average shop into a groper's paradise. In Nigeria the elections had produced a rash, not of posters, but of corrugated iron. Through jungle and desert, mountain and swamp, the country was littered with what appeared to be incongruously parked little road huts, stuck out in the wilds like sub-standard versions of the Tardis. They were actually voting booths. The general election preceding the handover of power by the military had been a necessarily complex operation. There had been 8,728 candidates and fifty political parties, later reduced to five. The ballot forms must have looked like an I.Q. test. Spread before the voter was a sort of Gnu and Guppy pâté whose constituent parts were indistinguishable to all but the most discriminatory palates. The One With The Difference, the G.N.P.P. was followed by the drably cloned N.P.N., U.P.N., N.P.P. and P.R.P. In the weeks that followed I often walked for hours simply recombining these letters in my head. I would, in my imagination, lead parties like P.U.R.N. or P.U.N.G. into the political arena, but I could never think of appropriate words to go behind the titles.

We drifted off towards the market area, stocking up on tea and semovita as we went. Semovita is useful stuff. It boils up easily into stodge for firsts or, with a bit of sugar and some powdered milk, it turns into slushy rice for pudding. Although there were few mosquitoes in the area, Mr. Bitrus suggested that we buy some mosquito coils to oppose the swarms that he assured us would be waiting further south. The coils were supposed to smoulder aromatically and get right up the most rapacious insect's nose. They were called "Golden Cock" and came from China. We reached the market place with our purchases. Somnolent traders lurked deep in shadows cast by music centres and cassette machines stacked dozens high in their polystyrene shells. Also for sale were less un-expected goods, gum arabic and lucky vultures' feet among them, but the sheer quantity of transistorised gear had been surprising.

"Only French cassette over in Niger," said Mr. Bitrus, "so

everybody buy Japan things here in this town." "Japan things" had been strongly discouraged by the French who still retain a very tight grip on their old West African colonies. From the vantage point of outer space these territories must look like industrial game reserves, protecting the rare but sputtering mobylette and the unique deux chevaux from Asiatic hordes on the boundaries. Mallam Fatori had therefore become something of an international bazaar, where the inhabitants of the eastern Sahara could obtain solace on magnetic tape, although in view of the noisome samples broadcast by the traders the physical purchase of a music machine seemed rather unnecessary. The most isolated desert dweller had only to muzzle his camel or his wife to pick up the strains of the Famous Felix Bros, toasts of Lagos, belting out across the sands.

Most villages in northern Nigeria have Koranic schools run by teachers known as "mallams", where children learn to read and write in Arabic and commit sections of the Holy Koran to memory. The sight of a class scribbling away or chanting verses by rote beneath a favourite tree is part of the fabric of northern life. A market stall offering the wooden tablets on which the children write brought a flood of reminiscence from Waz.

"Crikey," he said. It was a current word with him. "Haven't used one of these for years. Breaking in a new one's hard work. You have to really rub it down with sand for weeks to get it absolutely smooth." Waz had a habit of pulling in his lips every two or three sentences. When surprised he would make a sound halfway between "God" and "Guard". "Gar!" he continued. "Here's the ink. You have to make it up yourself from a mixture of acacia resin, like gum arabic, and powdered charcoal. We used to put sugar in ours because when we were ill we had to write special verses on our boards, then wash them off and drink them to get better." The thought of a row of small boys gargling back Koranic homilies sustained me through the rubbish and the turds as we wandered north out of the town towards the River Yobe. The sand was soft and

64

yielding and between them the sun and the goats had made an excellent start in eliminating the floral clutter consequent on the brief rains.

The river itself was about three minutes wade by camel from shore to shore and hump deep in the middle. The beasts revealing this intelligence had slopped across from the Niger side and emerged with dignity bedraggled as we reached the water's edge. We felt it something of an achievement to have at last arrived at our planned point of departure and Mr. Bitrus recorded the historic moment with a silly photo of Waz and me crouched "on our marks" in the river. Otherwise the send off could not have been described as riotous. One of the camels farted and a fisherman told us to get out of his light as he unhooked a sprat-like creature from his castnet. He threw a handful of maize into the water for bait and recast the net. We bought a few tilapia, common fish which resemble perch, and three small tiger fish whose ever ready fangs make real tigers look boringly herbivorous. As we sat cleaning the fish in the shade of a winterthorn a canoe full of women came over the water. They were dressed in typical Kanuri style, their anklelength cotton shifts with three-quarter sleeves worn over wrappers hitched above the breast. Standing up, these clothes give Kanuri women a wigwam shape and from a distance they look like a squad of pace sticks flapping along. The canoe was poled forward by a shrivelled gondolier in the standard white pyjama trousers and long shirt of the tropics, but his passengers positively fluoresced in their vividly dyed robes. It had occurred to me that all the water flowing past had to end up somewhere and so I made enquiries. The canoe man dashed my hopes of reviving the original plan of boating down to Baga by explaining that the river petered out into a swamp which began not far away and went on for ever.

With a final steadfast pose, captured by Mr. Bitrus, we took our first official steps south. The time was 10.04 hours and the date was Friday, 24 October. Since it was only three miles back to the fisheries compound our first day was easy, but passing a hut on the far side of the town, my shirt and a bag of ground

65

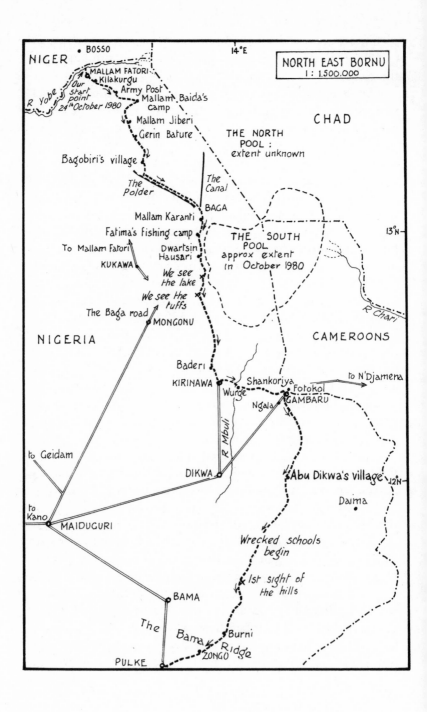

rice on my head, I felt a small hand clutch at my index finger. I did not look down although from the scurrying noises I deduced that a child had attached its grimy paw to mine.

"Where are you going?" it asked in husky English.

"Far," I said.

"Oh," said the child, and let go.

Back at the fisheries we gorged ourselves on fried onion and the tilapia. Despite our token start I did not want to proceed without a guide. Late in the afternoon I walked a couple of miles down the road to the Lake Chad Research Institute, a federal establishment, where I hoped to collect some up-to-the-minute facts about the lake. I particularly wanted climatic data. The base was well set out, with concrete roads and good shady bungalows, but, as the wall eyed clerk who met me explained, the rainfall statistics were a matter for "this offisal chanel" and not to be had. I was not very surprised. The officers of the institute were not "on seat", having sensibly buggered off to Maiduguri and points south, leaving the minions in command. I doubted that much information would have been divulged even if the officers had been "in post". My pessimism was founded on the cynical but realistic assumption that whoever had been appointed to read the meteorological instruments probably hadn't.

Strolling back through the monochromatic haze of evening I remembered that I had once taught English to a couple of fat Libyans, men whose capacity for food, drink and indolence was in no way inhibited by their vanity. I had nicknamed them the "Tummies". Being idle, the Tummies retained their linguistic virginity throughout the six month course. They began in a class for beginners and soon worked their way down to a special group, known as the Post Natal Squallers through whose ranks they effortlessly sank. Since their day-to-day requirements were fairly unsophisticated the Tummies had survived so far on smiles and mime until, having possibly been rejected once too often on the discotheque floor, they suddenly stopped grinning. They wobbled up to school one

67

day with what we took to be acute stomach aches, but their wild gestures indicated much more. "Kama Sutra meets Hara Kiri", suggested one wit. The secretaries became seriously worried and began to think in terms of straitjackets and the Samaritans but, in the nick of time, the Tummies' friends arrived and revealed all. Money being the least of their problems the Tummies were, apparently, desirous of a spot of cosmetic surgery to make them thin again. The operation is called an apronectomy and, after the necessary consultations, one Tummy had it done. He returned to Libya where, no doubt, he soon became his old self again and perhaps began to save up for another operation. The apronectomy saga led me to conclude that there is an aspect of human behaviour which I now call the Tummy Factor. I think of it as simply a tendency to purchase what is in fact best earned. In the Libyan's case a certain abstemiousness on the junk food front and even the odd press-up might, despite the effort, have served better than simply spending money.

I felt the Tummy Factor very strongly on the shores of Lake Chad. In the following weeks Waz and I walked south among a population of small-scale entrepreneurs, exploiting land and water with not much more than their own muscle power. What, I wondered, would they achieve with improved marketing and transport facilities, facilities which, compared to the grandiose schemes for canals and polders, would cost almost nothing? That, of course, was part of the problem. After all, an apronectomy sounds so much more impressive than a diet.

Waz's company gave me the confidence to face a journey whose potential for ruin by officialdom was enormous. Apart from the suspicions aroused by a white person actually "footing" anywhere in Nigeria, there was the standard visa problem to hurdle, followed by an interesting session of illegal immigration as Waz and I played hopscotch with the Cameroon border. He was in a sense my passbook, but this evening Waz was playing chef. As I arrived at Mr. Bitrus's house he was busy knocking up his first culinary effort of the journey, a delight of sardines, beans and rice, enlivened with a tin of Tomapep. Tomapep is a purée with a lot more pep than tom, and it comes in variously coloured tins according to potency. Waz had used the dreaded greenies which not only took off the roof of your mouth but had been known to blow holes in your underpants as well. Having doused ourselves as best we could, Mr. Bitrus led us to the nearby Kanuri hamlet of Kilakurgu.

The old towns of Bornu were built of sun baked bricks and adobe behind thick defensive walls, a style common to vast tracts of savannah country from Timbuctoo to the Sudan. In addition to this widespread pattern the Kanuri people have their own architectural style based on huts made entirely of grass, with intricate petticoats of thatch cascading from apex to floor. As we followed Mr. Bitrus past the outlying compounds it was apparent, even in the thin starlight, that Kilakurgu was about due for refurbishment. The huts were plonked on the bare sand like senile haystacks, silent but for the muted voices of villagers settling for the night. The headman, Sarkin Buluma Bukar Gambo, was waiting with a long silver torch of the type that corrodes on sight in Europe but remains for years a shiny and proud possession in the dryness of Bornu.

A moon of deepest apricot appeared, an unexpected face which found us huddled like insomniac pavement artists etching in the sand. The sarkin was explaining his ideas of where the lake had gone. Since no one but idiots and herdsmen walked when they could drive there was no longer an accepted footpath down to Baga but the sarkin had found a man prepared to chance his luck. His name was Jalo. Looking deep into his eyes I realised at once that Jalo was a normal human being about whom I knew nothing. Having been in similar situations before, I knew that hiring guides in the dark tended to be a hit and miss affair. Jalo appeared to have the right number of limbs and since the queue to join us was conspicuously short, we took him. One slight problem was that he spoke only

Kanuri and Waz, linguist though he was, knew very little. The other problem was that he wanted twice what I expected to pay, but since the whole trip had already passed the stage of financial lunacy, I agreed to his price. Having settled the domestic details we agreed to meet at dawn and went to bed.

8

Saturn, Jupiter and Venus synchronised their orbits perfectly for our farewell, twinkling like pinpricks through the eggshell tints of dawn. Jalo had arrived unsociably betimes, but had brought with him a floppy, plastic suitcase. He was evidently in ballast only. Rousing ourselves with glee, Waz and I unzipped the case and stuffed it full as a goose, stumbling blearily through the darkness in a disgraceful rush to unburden ourselves on our unsuspecting guide. Waz's radio was so ashamed of us that it peed all down its owner's arm, a flux of homemade lime juice having somehow soaked into the case on the journey up from Gulak. The vitamin infusion must have blown a fuse because the radio no longer worked, and so Waz left it behind for Mr. Bitrus who was still asleep. Slightly aggrieved about the lime juice but weeping crocodile tears over the radio I slipped into my plimsolls and set off after Jalo. Waz brought up the rear and three days later we reached Baga, our first sixty- or seventy-odd miles having induced in us a perverted sense of optimism. Being totally shagged out on arrival we felt that the remaining nine hundred miles between Baga and the Atlantic could be no worse, and that we would therefore make it. The little march had had its less-than-entertaining moments, but at least we had, as it were, turned the first sod.

We had carried plastic jerry cans of water. Floundering from tussock to tussock in pursuit of Jalo I sensed the gradual estrangement of my humerus from my scapula and I shifted the weight of water from hand to hand in the hope of a reconciliation. A refreshing south-easterly breeze gave us two hours of relatively cool walking from dawn until about eight o'clock, when the oven doors swung open. By this time I had solved my structural problems by drinking most of the water, but other irritations had arisen. My plimsolls, for example, had reinforced themselves substantially and as a distraction from the disagreeable sensation of trolling along with sandbags on my feet I pestered Jalo with questions about the trees. These all looked like variations on a theme of hawthorn, being a spiny mixture of Balanites, Zizyphus and Acacia senegalensis, but they were giving way quickly to low scrub land that had been, until quite recently, submerged knee-high in lake.

The ubiquitous sodom apple (*Calotropis persica*) became the tallest object on the landscape. It looked like a papier-mâché mock-up for the third day of creation, a crude piece of floral graffiti in the style of Henri Rousseau. The grass beneath was scratchy, low and dry, and from it grew emerald shrubs of *Salvadora persica*, frothing like exotic wigs through a threadbare yellow carpet. The salvadora bushes were choked with a pale green vine called *Leptadinia hastata* whose flowers, as our guide later demonstrated, made excellent tinder.

Jalo's brief was to lead us over the dry lake bed to Baga which, according to hours of complicated sums, I had calculated to be exactly fifty-one and three-quarter miles away on a bearing of 128° magnetic. On this first morning I continually checked our line of march with the compass and was continually disconcerted to find that Jalo knew nothing of 128° magnetic. He appeared to be heading straight for Peking and we were obviously going to walk rather more than fifty-one and three-quarter miles. Rather than succumb to acute scout-mastership, I let my interest in navigation wane and as the day progressed I simply looked forward to arriving, wherever it might be.

Signs of passing cattle were littered for miles along our way and just before midday we found ourselves surrounded. The scrub had been replaced by a tangle of half burnt reeds, rooted in what appeared to be brown soot. Hundreds of thin cows nodded past steadily, their superb horns working the horizon like cranes above a busy dock. Although the cows were walking slowly, their effect on the friable alluvium was roughly that of heavy cavalry on a powder puff, and we were instantly smothered in dust.

"Mobber," said Jalo. Mobbers are one of eight or ten subdivisions within the Kanuri nation. Jalo himself was a Suerti Kanuri from Geidam in western Bornu, but the cows belonged to a pastoral family of Mobber Kanuri, through whose area we were now passing. The beasts were of a strain called Buduma. They are the humpless descendants of the Hamitic longhorn. This was one of the earliest breeds of cattle to penetrate West Africa, and its characteristics are also preserved in the Andalusian cattle of Spain and the famous longhorns of the Wild West. Cowboys, however, were not noted family men and would, I am sure, have looked askance at the fleet of donkeys bobbing along like lobster pots on the upwind flank of the herd. Rows of little Mobbers were perched among the rolls of mats and the big round gourds strapped like kettle drums to panniers slung over the donkeys' backs. A whole Mobber family was on the hoof, moving further out on to the dry lake bed for new grazing. The men followed up on foot, some in tightly wound turbans, others carrying bows or short whips of rawhide. Kicking up its own dusty smokescreen, the drive proceeded in remarkable silence. We continued with the herd until we passed an established camp where we stopped to greet the family head who was known to Jalo.

Alhaji Shari emerged from a flimsy shelter of corn stalks, cardboard and goat skins to greet us. Like most Kanuri males his head was shaved and his skin was profoundly black. He was barefooted and wore the usual long cotton shirt and loose trousers. A dozen calves were tethered beside the shelters but the main herd was out in the bush with the al Haji's herdboys. Sitting in the shade with a calabash of milk between us I nudged Waz.

"Ask him how many cows he's got," I said.

"Better not do that," said Waz, "it's like asking a stranger about his bank account. I'll just tell him you're interested in cows because your old man used to keep them."

The al Haji probably had upwards of four hundred head. Meat is expensive stuff in Nigeria and at current exchange rates he was worth about £150,000, although his domestic assets, scattered about in the form of frayed mats and old pots, might only have grossed a fiver. I remembered the incredulity of Ernest the soft drinks man. Why, indeed, were Peugeots not parked behind the corn stalks? Why didn't the al Haji simply flog off his cows and retire to the nearest condominium? Questions of this sort presuppose a commercial attitude which is not yet established among the pastoralists of Bornu. They are not so much cattle breeders as cattle people. Their beasts do not convert so easily into cash. The herds are a form of social currency, evolving with the herdsmen and their families, a human warp and a bovine woof, each sustaining the other over the unfolding cloth of generations.

The al Haji offered us more milk from a large, pumpkin shaped gourd, decorated with bark fibre. Everything in the camp seemed to be greased and worn with age, including the al Haji's senior wife who happened to be present. Kanuri women suffer the double misfortune of being rather ugly themselves, while having absolutely stunning neighbours in the Shuwa and Fulani people with whom they share north-eastern Bornu. Being almost belligerently religious, Kanuri seem to lack the spontaneity of their less orthodox neighbours. They like their women to remain at home, preferably behind the compound wall. In the bush and in the smaller villages the exigencies of life force women out to the fields and the wells, but higher up the social scale wives tend to live in some degree of purdah.

Kanuri women are generally rather lumpy in build, and their somewhat pugnacious "Kanuri look" is enhanced by facial scars whose central feature is a wide, raised cicatrisation which dips like a ski jump from the hairline, over the brow and right down the nose. Despite their natural disadvantages, or perhaps because of them, Kanuri ladies somehow exude a suburban complacency and are groomed to bourgeois perfection. Their hairstyles are particularly striking, tight and neat, gathered well off the neck and braided into a central cock's comb with a surrounding fringe. The several variations are Mesozoic in style, evocative of the age of giant reptiles, although there are some creations with a hint of the Trojan war helmet about them. So as not to disturb their crinite elaborations Kanuri women tend to carry their loads on the nape of the neck, proceeding even under empty calabashes with their heads bowed forward submissively, a line of female Atlases on pillar duty.

Being pastoralists, Alhaji Shari and his family were atypical of the Kanuri as a whole who are basically an agricultural people, sharing ideas about religion, social organisation and subsistence patterns with many of the other peoples of the western savannahs. The Kanuri sense of history, however, tends to be stronger than that of their neighbours. Traditions are recorded both orally and in written chronicles which list the doings of kings and princes, but do not say much about the everyday facts of life.

Long ago, in the days of the Venerable Bede, Muslims advancing across North Africa had overrun Spain and were pushing up into France. They might even have reached Britain and put an end to Bede's mission had they not been repulsed at the battle of Tours in A.D. 732. The same outward push by the Arabs had produced a westward movement of non-Muslims from south-western Arabia. These people crossed the Red Sea and gradually pushed on through the Sudan and across Central Africa. Some of them eventually emerged as top dogs in an area bordering the north shore of Lake Chad. There they established the Sefuwa dynasty which actually lasted over a thousand years, and its successor still survives in the person of the Shehu of Bornu. The first Sefuwa king to accept Islam succeeded to the throne just as the Domesday Book was appearing, a "some you win, some you lose" situation since the Muslims had been kicked out of Toledo the previous year.

By about 1200 the Sefuwa ruling family had become integrated with the local population in the same way that the Normans and the Saxons were mingling, and in 1193 the first black king took the throne of the empire which had then become known as Kanem. The Sefuwas shifted their base of operations south into Bornu in the fifteenth century and built a capital not far from present day Mallam Fatori. High noon for Kanem-Bornu came under the rule of Mai Idriss Alooma, who died in the same year as Good Queen Bess. Mai Idriss was by all accounts an exceptionally brilliant man. His fame spread to Cairo, where regular lodging houses were established for Bornuese pilgrims, and to Tunis where firearms were obtained for his army. A gradual decline in power and influence over the next two hundred years culminated in the sacking of the capital by a Fulani army. This happened in the same year that the Pope excommunicated Napoleon, namely 1809. The Fulanis were beaten off but the dynasty fell and was replaced by another which lasted only forty-seven years until, in 1893, a slave dealer from the Sudan crossed the River Shari with his private army and wiped out the Bornuese cavalry at a stroke. The slaver's name was Rabeh and he looked all set to begin a third dynasty from his new capital at Dikwa when, on 22 April 1900, he was killed at the battle of Kusseri by the French, who had taken the lessons of the Hundred Years War to heart and had abandoned knights in armour for field pieces and a gunboat called the *Léon Blot*.

In accordance with the "lucky dip" Treaty of Berlin, Bornu was divided between the United Kingdom and Germany. The Germans lost their bit during the First World War and Britain ran the show through the traditional administrative structure until 1960 when the independent nation of Nigeria was launched.

Like the feudal barons of Europe, the Bornuese ruling families had two main sources of wealth. First, there was war, which produced tribute, booty and slaves, and second, taxes could be levied on the peasants themselves who could also be recruited as soldiers. The Empire of Bornu had certain in common with the feudal stages of British history, including the use of chainmail, but, unlike medieval England, no wool trade or manufacture developed to drag society forward, nor later did revised forms of worship emerge to challenge the established matrix of Islamic life. Islamic principles of submission and obedience are similar in style to medieval Christianity in which, as the historian Barbara Tuchman has noted, "the life of the spirit and of the afterworld was always superior to the here and now, to material life on earth." She goes on to say in her book *A Distant Mirror* that, "the rupture of this principle and its replacement by belief in the worth of the individual and of an active life not necessarily focused on God is, in fact, what created the modern world and ended the Middle Ages."

Despite the manoeuvrings of Empire, the mass of the Bornu population continued much as it always had done; that is, it grew food, raised stock, praised the Lord and bred. The economy remained virtually unchanged in both organisation and technology until well into this century, and even today is based largely on primary agricultural production, despite the icing of invested national funds.

We were two hours south of Alhaji Shari's camp when we hit the army. Bits of combat gear were strung up between half a dozen bell tents which had been erected on slightly rising ground. A couple of men were lounging beneath an awning. Dressed in civvies, they exuded the malevolent unpredictability of bored Tonton Macoutes, deckchairing away a Sunday afternoon.

"Shit," I thought.

We tried to look inconspicuous but they called us over and began the routine display of aggression that I had come to expect from government backed muscle.

"What you parmet?" the larger one kept shouting. "What you from?"

Jalo faded offstage and I kept up an ingratiating smile until Waz arrived. Both he and the ranting soldier had similar

tribal scars raked across their cheeks. By a great stroke of
good luck the ranter was actually a Marghi and even knew
Waz's father. We were home and dry, and within half-an-
hour were burrowing into a mound of tuwo. I was presented
with a fresh pack of Benson and Hedges and the soldiers
drifted off for a siesta, leaving Waz and me at the crude
desk to survey the sporadic traffic along the track which led
towards the Chadian border. The lake was expected back in
a few months' time, but until then there were herds of cattle
and crops of maize for the populace to tend out on the exposed
lake bed.

As we prepared to leave in the mid-afternoon there was an
ugly scene. A group of Fulani youths wandered by but made
the mistake of neglecting obeisance to the tin gods, who had
returned to their table. The Fulanis were duly screamed at and
one was grabbed and dragged over the awning. After a great
deal of shouting and a few cuffs round the head the youths
were released minus a pocketful of naira. The trouble with
bullies is that they usually win and I made no move to inter-
vene, confining myself to a light but frustrated grinding of the
molars. If not for Waz's connections it could easily have been
us at the receiving end of the soldiers' tantrums.

A lance-corporal asked me if I knew his senior brother
whose name was David Jacob and who had gone to England in
1966. "Mek you snap my picher, de time you return back for
your country say you give um," he said. I did, and, Mr. David
Jacob, I have your junior brother's picher.

That afternoon we made the error of leaving the beaten track.
Within ten minutes we were blundering through a twelve-
foot-high tangle of rushes and sedge which combined the
abrasive qualities of sandpaper with the sliceability of razor
blades in a vigorously welcoming caress. Escaping from one
vegetable prison we immediately entered another, a field of
the dreaded *Cenchrus biflorus*, or cramcram grass. Cramcram
is to your everyday verdant pasture what the Chinese water
torture is to a Jacuzzi—sheer hell. The burrs are like minute,

magnetic hedgehogs with spines of finest glass—biological warfare and should be banned under the Geneva Convention. They get absolutely everywhere. Jalo said something. Waz translated.

"He says that this is why the Kanuris are circumcised."

"Tres drôle," I said. "Tell him I'm surprised they're not all castrated as well."

Picking ourselves free we hit another track and were suddenly into a superb prairie of feathery green grass. We could see for miles and made our way towards an isolated hut. The owner was one of the thousands of cultivators who move on to the lake bed in the dry season. He presented us with a bundle of freshly pulled peanut vines from which we each picked a handful of soft shells. In 1964 peanuts, with cocoa, made up half the value of Nigeria's exports. Africa's most populous country lived until the late 1960s on an income largely derived from the sale of peanuts, cocoa and palm oil of which, in 1964, Nigeria produced twenty-one per cent of the total world harvest. In 1980 Nigeria was a net importer of all these things. Jalo interviewed our benefactor and we strode on, confident of his directions which, of course, led us directly back into the appalling undergrowth.

We had about an hour of daylight left when we heard a far-off bleat. Tunnelling through my pack for a pair of binoculars I made out several white blobs towards which we struggled. We were hoping to get directions from the owners who would not be far away. Approaching the blobs, which were rustling about on the outskirts of an abandoned farm plot, I realised that the exertions of the day spent under a hot sun had driven me insane. Milling about with surprising nonchalance were several hundred ovine rears. They had no fronts. They simply ceased to exist forrard of the thorax. Oh my God. Were we approaching a black hole? Or had there been a cock-up at a pantomime? Fully prepared for an "Oh yes they are, Oh no they aren't" routine with the truncated sheep I followed Jalo through the fading light. As we grew closer it slowly became apparent that the sheep were, after all, complete. Great relief. Their front ends were entirely black and had been invisible in the grainy evening haze. They were large, floppy eared creatures of a distinct breed called Uda, which is also the name of the Fulani people associated with them. Two shepherd boys watched us plonk down our bags between a small waterhole and a dilapidated shelter. They were Uda Fulanis from across the border in Niger, and were very "bush" according to Waz. They spoke an archaic form of the language, studded with "Thee"s and "Thou"s. Fulani speaking people are found right across West Africa from Senegal to Cameroon and although the dialects vary they are mutually intelligible.

Waz was rather suspicious of the boys but, unless the sheep themselves were killers, the situation seemed quite peaceful to me. At least the boys had the good manners not to laugh at my farcical camp craft. I wanted to set a good, self-disciplined example to Jalo and Waz on this, our first night in the bush. Unfortunately I fell into the shallow waterhole. The sides had crumbled as I stopped to fill the pot. Muddy and wet I set the pot on a hastily scraped-up fire and began to string the mosquito nets to the shelter. I must have nudged a key section of rot. The whole thing rocked slightly then collapsed on my head. By this time Jalo and Waz were rocking slightly, too. Brushing powdered cellulose from my hair I turned to attend the steaming pot, tripped on a log, spilt most of the water over my rucksack and scalded my feet with the rest. "Bloody marvellous," I thought. At this stage a third Fulani appeared and after some discussion we gathered up our things, extracted our nets from the wreckage of the shelter and followed in a tide of sheep to the Fulanis' sleeping place.

There was nothing very special about it, but the Udas had a mallam from the nearest permanent settlement visiting them. The sheep were suffering from an undiagnosed problem and the mallam had been asked to help. He was a holy man, for which the Fulani term is "modibbo". The Fulani people have produced a disproportionately large number of these divines, many of them men of great influence in the states of West

Africa. The majority, however, operate at village level, combining a normal peasant life with a religious "practice", and function variously as holy man, doctor and scribe.

Without a sacerdotal hierarchy in the Christian sense, the vast majority of Muslim priests live lives indistinguishable from the communities of which they are part, indeed the very title, "priest", implies a degree of separation wholly foreign to Muslim tradition. The Muslim world has its share of saints and schisms but it remains a remarkably free and inclusive Church. It always surprises me to think that the democracy of which the West is so proud has flourished with arrangements for the spirit left in such manifestly undemocratic hands.

The presence of Mallam Baida, sleeping out in the vegetable chaos of the lake to pray for sick and dying sheep, seemed to personify the essentially encompassing nature of Islam. We in the West appear to be moving towards the complete secularisation of all life. We tend to divorce things from spiritual principles, but in many parts of the world this is not yet the case. To Muslims, for example, the distinction between the sacred and the profane, between Caesar and God, is blurred and almost meaningless, and in Africa, whether Muslim, pagan or anything else, people seem to have a pervading sense of God which is markedly absent in the West. The spiritual difference that is discernible between Africans and Europeans is very difficult to put into words which do not sound trivial or condescending, but I quote the scholar Seyyed Hossien Nasr:

It might be said that most of the discussion in the West concerning freedom involves in one way or other the freedom to do or to act, whereas in the context of traditional man the most important form of freedom is the freedom to be, to experience pure existence itself. This is the most profound form of freedom but it is nearly completely forgotten today because modern man who is so fond of collecting experiences has ceased to remember what the experience of pure existence . . . means.

81

"Bismillahi," said Mallam Baida. "In the name of God." A bowl of rice and soup had materialised from the darkness, brought over by one of the boys from the Udas' main camp about two miles away. Squatting round the bowl we ate.

"Alhamdullilahi," said a satisfied Jalo, rocking back on his heels and sucking his teeth. "Alhamdullilahi" means "God be praised".

"Thank the mallam very much," I said to Waz. Baida said something in reply.

"He says God has brought you here and you are welcome," said Waz. He and Mallam Baida talked at length in soft twitterings of Fulani. It so happened that Gulak village required another Koranic teacher and Waz mentioned the vacancy. The mallam said that he might well travel down that way when the Gulak district head returned from Mecca.

An intensely bright shooting star flared across the sky. I lay in the chirruping matrix of frogs and noisy insects, reviewing our first day, comparing the intense frustrations of the undergrowth with the pleasure of being here with the Udas. It wasn't a pleasure for long. The night was absolutely freezing. I spent most of it tending a sulky fire of ambatch, a tree with half the density of cork. It actually grows in the lake and is good for making rafts and floats but useless as a fuel; since the next nearest tree was about ten miles away I had to make do with it.

We ran out of ambatch well before dawn and struggled to boil our morning tea on a fire of maize husks which, as a heat source, behaved like unconscious glow worms. After sloshing down a little lukewarm semovita we followed the Udas, who led us to what they had decided was the relevant track. They rattled off a list of the villages that we should pass through. After a couple of miles we realised that we were travelling off the lake bed and would soon be following the old shore line. We passed by golden dumps of bean-hard maize. Since rain was not expected for another nine months there was no great hurry about moving the grain. The threshing was a women-and-children job and was done by taking a cob in one hand and hitting it with a stick held in the other. Spurning the short measure European method of securing sacks by gathering at the neck and tying off, the Bornu maize growers strain the hessian with a teetering meniscus of grain before sewing on large flaps of extra sacking. Thus filled the sacks weigh about two hundredweight apiece and are transported by camel to the nearest vehicle track.

I asked how people could tell exactly where their old plots were, once the lake had receded for another year. I imagined that they perhaps did it like frogs, returning to their natal ponds, only in reverse.

"They tell by natural features," said Waz, after consulting with Jalo. I looked around.

"What natural features?" I said. Other than the vegetation, which in any case floated away on the lake during each inundation, features of any sort were in short supply. The only ones that we had seen so far that morning were a few overgrown canoes. Further discussions caused Waz to stop and wave his arms expansively.

"All these natural features have names," he said. "They're called after the pioneers." During the past decade large numbers of Hausa-speaking people from north-central Nigeria have emigrated to the lake area in search of fish and better farming land. From villages established on permanently dry sites they move out to cultivate the lake bed as the water recedes, planting a variety of crops, although maize predominates. Being simply built, of poles, grass mats and corn stalks, whole settlements can be taken to bits and moved great distances within a day. Unhindered by livestock and with the help of vehicles, the immigrants respond to the changing lake level with great flexibility and at absolutely no expense to the taxpayer. The same cannot be said of the Quixotic wheat growing schemes.

I plodded on across the "natural features", my curiosity unsatisfied. Once, in pre-dental limbo, I had read about the ancient Polynesians who, according to the dog-eared article, could tell roughly where they were by holding impromptu sea-water tastings as they sailed along. The best of them would take a swill and say something like, "Hmm, frightful presumption but only a fruity league or so south-west of Krakatoa", and with three rousing cheers they would make another perfect landfall. Perhaps the Bornu people went round stuffing themselves with earth as Lake Chad dried up, making comments like, "Ah, tastes like Fred's place, mine can't be far away."

A through train of wind soughs briefly in the leafless thorn. It sounds like dead snakes dancing and a dog barks in the splintering heat. The noise is baffled through huge, bread-oven silences and dies in the hot, yielding sand. A girl sings absently beside a well, a plainsong bleached and white for minds bemused in the hot monotony. There is no conversation but we do occasionally say things. Jalo suddenly asks Waz how long it is since Tafawa Balewa died. Neither man looks up, neither checks his stride.

"Er, fifteen years, two months, ten days," says Waz. He isn't joking.

"Oh, fifteen years, two months, ten days," says Jalo.

"Yeah," says Waz.

A Toyota billows past, fast moving fruit. I'm tempted.

We stop at a Hausa settlement called Mallam Jiberi, borrow a mat and move into the shade. We know it is a Hausa village because of the little girls. They wear wrappers to their waists then loose fitting bodices and their heads are lost endearingly in kerchiefs. Hausa girls are often betrothed at six or seven and brought up in the household of the prospective husband. Even the smallest have an adult gravity. Those now coming towards us average out at four foot nothing, but display the natural elegance of poplars as they approach with bright enamelware on trays which never, ever fall. Lowering their dishes and removing lids we see that they have brought us deep fried bean cakes and small bowls of ground spices. The little girls sit waiting, not like sales persons at all, until, satisfied, we fall back to sleep. They take their pennies and go.

We doze through the call to prayer at two o'clock, the salat al azzuhr. The muezzin's cry is our alarm—Awake! For sunshine in the burning day has cooled enough to recommence our way—apologies to Omar Khayyám.

"Allahaaaa ak'bar," the voice shimmers, "Allahaaaa ak'bar, La illaha illa Llah . . ." Beautiful, mesmeric sound, I have heard it a thousand times. "Allah ak'bar, God is great. I testify to the oneness of God, La illaha illa Llah." This essential creed of Islam, called the shahada, rolls through the heat. Yes, there is no god but God, no divinity but The Divine.

Yes. Or no. It's still so hot.

We roll up the mat and leave. At the end of the afternoon we reach another conglomerate of grass and corn stalks called Gerin Bature. That means "white man's town" in Hausa, but the headman is a Suerti Kanuri, the same as Jalo. His name is Buluma Modari and he brings us water, brackish and slightly salty as it has been at all the wells today. Two small carpets are laid. Waz and Jalo are to sleep on gypsies in vivid tarantella and I get an abstract disaster in brushed nylon. Much later Buluma Modari brings maize meal and a soup of butter.

"We don't really have headmen in Europe, do we?" says Waz, and realising that there is a lot more to that than meets the eye we fall asleep.

On the third morning of our walk we reached a track with double ruts that cut directly into spindly thorn breaks. I had seen this particular stretch of vegetation before. There were no turbans nor any shawls caught up in the branches, but, after a few more miles, the depressing fact that we were back on the road by which we had come sank into our loads.

Two women were coming towards us with large gourds and what looked like the week's ironing balanced on their heads. On closer inspection the laundry turned out to be folded headcloths, and I saw that both women were scuffling along in nasty, laceless, men's style shoes. From these plastic sabots, travelled shins emerged, and long flamingo limbs. Wrists and arms swung slim as gibbons, boned in porcelain and brittle willow, and the sordid footwear was somehow overridden. The women were indelibly Fulani: Borroro'en, the purest of the race, the ones least amenable to a sedentary life who still follow the "Fulani way", called laawol pulaaku in their language. To a stranger, pulaaku has its outward expression in the characteristic demeanour of the bush Fulani, variously described as aloof, proud, arrogant, disdainful or even shy. Borroro are certainly restrained in their behaviour.

Unlike the Shuwas and the pastoral sections of the Kanuri people the bush Fulanis do not really have a tribal territory, but have wandered like a mist across the savannahs. They prefer to marry among themselves, ideally to a first cousin, so preserving the moral purity of the clan round which life revolves. Despite their customary endogamy they have mingled with local populations and can be completely Negroid in appearance, though they most admire a light skin colour, coppery, not "red" like Europeans, a slight bone structure and straight hair, thin lips, and, above all, a long, narrow nose. The women, especially, have a gypsy look about them, their crinkly pigtails hanging down at the temple like Hassidic payot, or curling out beneath bright headscarves and silver rings, suggesting perhaps that fiddlers and a dancing bear might not be far behind.

Many theories exist purporting to explain the origin of the Fulani people, but what is generally accepted is that their ancestors entered Africa from the Middle East (some say India), and migrated along the North African coast. They turned south through Morocco and the western Sahara to occupy parts of Senegal and present-day Guinea. From about the eleventh century onwards they dispersed eastwards between the desert to the north and the tsetse fly to the south, eventually reaching the northern Cameroons and parts of Chad. Settled Fulanis established ruling houses in many of the city states of Hausa land, and from Sokoto they swept across the north in Holy conquest which just failed to subdue Bornu. The great Fulani jihad of the early nineteenth century was a movement of

Islamic revival rather than reform, leading the faithful back to their roots and, incidentally, much enriching the successful generals. Paradoxically, the bush Fulanis were left in their semi-pagan state, many being at best only nominally Muslim even today, their "bush" ways at odds with the sophistications of statecraft and city life.

Waz stopped the women in plastic shoes as they passed by. "Pullo," he called softly. Pullo is just the singular for Fulani. The women turned, graceful as whippets. The milk which they had for sale was a couple of days old and it tasted like kippers washed in lemon juice, but it eased the midday heat. Lurking flocculations of butter bounced gently on my lips while my tongue explored the textures of the calabash, soft end-grain inside, the outer suface reflectively smooth. As we sat drinking we were brushed by the shadows of an old man and a squirrel-grey donkey. A goat was folded into a side pannier, its throat a slash of uncongealed vermilion, bright against the washed-out haze.

Resting through the hours of zealous heat, we met a man called Amadu Bagobiri. He was about fifty years old, with silver grizzle on his chin and a solid ring of silver on his hand. He had emigrated ten years ago from Madagali, in Waz's home district, and he brought us a bowl of gruel. He apologised as he set it down. He was sorry, he said, but his wife had died. Otherwise we would be having the best meal that a poor man could afford. He had, he said, sold all his sheep to pay for her local treatment, but it hadn't worked and she had eventually died in the mission hospital at Lassa, of the fever fame.

"Then I came here," said Bagobiri. "When I first arrived I discovered that the people were fishing. I mean I came to farm and I didn't understand what they were doing. So I wanted to leave that very afternoon but they gave me a place to make a farm. The land is free. I planted in moist ground. It gets muddy when the lake has gone. When the harvest came I got twenty-five bags of maize. I was so surprised I decided to stay.

The best thing about this place is there's no weeding and for two weeks' work you could get fifty bags of maize. I planted about two kilos of groundnuts and I got twenty-three sacks, and I only had to work ten hours planting sweet potatoes and I got twelve sacks. Some years you get three crops. She died in Ramadan. It's a good time. The gate of heaven opens a bit wider."

Our shadows were growing rubbery. It was sundown and we found ourselves still walking, when, all of a sudden, we reached the Polder. I felt like the monkey in *2001*, all set to touch this weird intrusion and start flinging bones around, thus establishing a new civilisation (national anthem—also sprach Zarathustra of course). I digress. The track was banked up and over the Polder and continued into the bush on what we presumed was a long sweep round to Baga. Since the Polder ran with scarcely a kink straight into Tim's backyard we decided to follow it. Thirty-six kilometres, he had said, and with a bit of luck we were already some way along it. Waz reckoned halfway, but after ten minutes we came to a marker with "Kilometre 34" painted on it. We were all rather hoping that the next marker would say "Hallo! The End," but it didn't. It said "Kilometre 32". Oh well.

We continued. It would be quicker than following the road, and being eight feet above the bush we were on the scenic route, although the view did not last long because it was nearly bed time and getting dark. Our main problem was water. Although we had a little, there were no villages nor any wells ahead where we could replenish our supply. I assumed that since we were travelling at night we would be less thirsty than usual but I was completely wrong about this. We bowled along quite happily for the first few kilometres with the starlit bush beneath us and camp fires twinkling for miles on both sides. We heard the padded stirrings of cattle gathered for the night, and, occasionally, the caustic snores of sleepy donkeys shattered the stillness.

The night developed and uncomfortable reality crept over

us. Walking in a dead straight line became extremely boring, and then rather painful. I had blisters and Waz had bad stomach cramps. We all had mosquitoes. Having walked all day we were rather tired but the winged pests kept us going until, at about nine o'clock, Waz groaned and had to stop. The mosquitoes dropped like vultures at a barbeque. Jalo wrapped Waz up in a net and I jumped off the Polder to scout round for some fuel. I tossed up a few sticks then realised that without magnetic boots I could not get back myself. The iron pilings were impossible to climb. I caught the exotic whiff of smouldering mosquito coils lit by Jalo. Swathed in his net, he leant over to help me up. "Balcony scene," I thought, falling back into the scrub. "Chief Houri meets Childe Harolde." I made it on the third attempt and Jalo hauled me up. We had a brew and set off again, but Waz was in great discomfort and we finally had to stop for several hours. Jalo and I shared a net, sitting back to back, the corners propped up with our knees. We looked like Siamese ghosts. The mosquitoes were desperate. My skin felt like Crimean turf with the six hundred doing their thing all over it. The bastards were trampling me to pieces, but at least I didn't have tummy ache—yet. Waz recovered slightly and we continued, eventually reaching the end of the Polder as horizontal purples were blooming in the sky. The Greek and his dredger had gone, but Tim had not and we collapsed in a sweaty heap at his door.

Despite Tim's open-handed generosity, the insect ridden intimacies of the previous night were frozen in the European house. Jalo was obviously uneasy in the strange machine which with its plumbing and electrics was technologically novel, and, with its rooms and doors, was socially unknown. Tim's house was more than just an ordered extension of the world of grass and earth outside. It broke with the existing order altogether. It had straight lines and square, smooth walls, and it worked in special ways. Ostensibly the European lived inside it, though actually the house lived inside him. No wonder Jalo felt so awkward in this hall of foreign symbols.

A local man who worked for Tim took Jalo as his guest. His compound was nearby.

We had hired Jalo to accompany us only as far as Baga. Waz and I both liked him and, now that we had arrived, we asked him to come with us round the southern end of the lake to Gambaru on the Cameroon border. He had agreed, partly because we would still be in Kanuri country and partly because he wanted the money, but mostly because we were going to buy a donkey. I, for one, am not keen on rucksacks, and if I can persuade some poor dumb creature to carry my stuff for me so much the better.

We hosed ourselves down then breakfasted and Jalo dumped his gear in the compound of Tim's chap. We then went donkey hunting and scoured the unpaved sandpit of a town for several hours. Waz and Jalo followed up the leads while I lurked in the background, a sort of "Mr. Big" in shorts. I really should have worn reflecting sunglasses or turned up my lapels because Nigerian markets get a little bullish with white skins in on the deal. We tracked down a likely specimen just after midday but Jalo blew the gaff by inadvertently telling the owner that I was the prospective buyer. I could have bought an E-type Jag with what the old man subsequently asked. He was an avaricious creature, with teeth like mildewed skittles and orange stains of kola on his lips. He was far, far uglier than the gnarled old donkey tethered in his yard. After tense negotiations we settled on a price of gross proportions, a ransom ten times the sum which I had paid on a previous donkey assisted passage through East Africa. Skittle teeth had got about twice the local rate out of me. The sly old bugger must have known all about rucksacks, but the donkey seemed all right, although he looked a bit depressed and needed some chiropody. Waz put him into gear and I squatted knowledgeably to check his stride. That our donkey was a "he" I was left in no doubt. Between his legs he had a pair of battered ovals, hanging like the hard won souvenirs of a rugby football tournament and wrapped in something like a size ten teabag. It was an astounding sight.

Our noble steed was ninety-nine per cent pure testicle and from the piles of dung about the yard I assumed the rest was into food processing. He did not have a name but, since Waz was ploughing through *I Claudius* at the time, we called him Claude. He had a down-at-heel, "it's-me-piles, guv" sort of expression and I summed him up as middle-aged and strongly unionised. He cost me roughly fifty quid.

We spent the rest of the day and the following morning on what the army calls "personal admin"—clipping toenails, washing clothes, mending and the like, and we went into Baga once again to buy some hardware, specifically a mobile kitchen unit. Geologically speaking Bornu is a bad place for the caring chef to be. It is a stoneless land where, had the fancy taken them, the Philistines could have ruled the roost without sneaky little shepherd boys socking them in the forehead. Not an ounce of ammo for miles, and, of course, nothing big enough for cooking stones until the mountains started. Setting up a cooking fire without stones is a bit like losing your car keys, irritating at first but swiftly productive of blasphemous outbursts. Ingeniously cantilevered pots either spill, or settle with a tarry sizzle into the ashes. All food begins to taste like burning liquorice. We therefore bought an old kerosene can and hit it until we had a satisfactory fire box. We also got a sleeping mat each and we bought Claude his harness. He was not exactly overwhelmed with this gift. The panniers were floppy netting baskets made of twisted reeds and his pack saddle was a retired sack stuffed with straw. We also bought lengths of bark-fibre rope, and having thanked Tim for having us, set off for Kirinawa, fifty or so miles away on the bottom left-hand corner of the lake. We would be skirting the south pool which, we heard, had started to rise.

Waz and Jalo took it upon themselves to load Claude. I more or less knew what would happen and of course it did, several times, but I felt that the hour-and-a-half they eventually spent pursuing our gear round Claude's unshapely body was a reasonable price for lesson number one. I then demonstrated the Pern method of loading and Claude staggered off like a bondage freak on the Pennine Way, completely lost under a mountain of stuff which all fell off as Tim was doing the goodbye photos. Restraining Waz from using a welding torch we fixed the loads in one more go. Claude looked unbelievably pissed off.

9

The sun was turning home by the time we had managed to leave Baga. We had been given careful directions by a local game guard. "Straight through the trees," he had said, "then over the cattle tracks, ignore all the other tracks, then across open ground till you see two really big trees and that's Mallam Karanti. Ask the headman if you can sleep in his compound."

The three miles took us just over two hours and when we finally did arrive we could still see the crane derricks left over from the Polder scheme. They were poking above the trees into an overcast sky and oddly enough they looked part of the natural landscape. The reason for our slow progress was a stretch of cramcram grass about five hundred yards wide. Jalo made his stupid circumcision joke again but was quietly upstaged by Claude who, somewhere in the first few rods, poles or perches of cramcram did what came to be known as a "Houdini".

"Claude's done a Houdini," said Waz, and so he had, having somehow turned his entire load through 180°. Our baggage was now competing with Claude's previously described parts for the limited space between his legs, and it was losing. We reloaded quickly but it took us days to pick the cramcram off. However, relief was at hand because, though we hardly noticed it, we were slowly moving into a different vegetation zone in which kinder grasses grew. The sahel zone, through which we had been walking was gradually giving way to Sudan savannah. At Kirinawa the annual average rainfall is double that of Mallam Fatori, and the rainfall would continue to increase sharply as we moved south, although since the rains were everywhere finished for the year we would see none of it.

Claude ended the walking day with a sardonic grin and an erection. This last, somewhat vulgar, display turned out to be a regular late afternoon habit with him. Apart from the horrible stretch of cramcram we had been lucky enough to have had most of our way already burnt off and so we were all rather sooty as we sat round a bowl of millet goo and baobab leaf soup kindly provided by the headman. He left us with a couple of buckets of water to wash with and, crawling under my net, I went to sleep. Waz said that I often laughed in my sleep. Perhaps it was to make up for my frequent sense of humour failures in the daytime.

I knocked up a little breakfast while Jalo sulked under his net with his rosary until, emerging wearily, he took Claude to the nearest well for a drink. Despite our warning fire of dung and straw, and the customary daylight truce, the mosquitoes nibbled on because, said Jalo, mosquitoes were afraid of nothing but the sun, which today was hidden by thick grey clouds. As we left the village there was a tremendous slanging match coming from the next compound between a man and his wife. A couple of other women joined in and the last words were "Right, wait till we get to the in-laws." The vast majority of Kanuri marriages end in divorce and it sounded as if this one was following the usual pattern.

Soon after leaving Mallam Karanti we were again in a tall reed bed and again we could hear the sounds of cattle moving all around us. This time it was a Fulani herd of white sanga, their swinging dewlaps and firm shoulder humps swollen with fat after the abundance of the rainy season. The children of the family went by on donkeys as had the smaller Mobbers. One little girl was cradling a lamb. A wrinkled granny picked her way over the reeds with a long stick to help her and her headload secured in a net. Looming through the dust at the rear came the family patriarch mounted on a camel and beneath him the whistling herdboys kept the drive going with their cries. Like us, they were heading for Gambaru and the Cameroons, and for a moment I considered joining them. They were, however, planning to take the journey slowly and would not be arriving for two months, by which time we hoped to be through the Mandara Mountains and over the River Benue.

The day was shadowless, industrially grey, and dusty from the harmattan which had now begun to blow. We came across a fishing camp just after what would have been elevenses, had we any buns or lime juice left. We stopped. The grass had been burnt off in all directions, exposing earth both fledgling bald and bare. We hobbled and unloaded Claude whose shins were bleeding from mosquito bites. He hopped off uncomplainingly to browse the rude grass shelters put up by the fishermen, a tolerant lot who shooed him away quite mildly. Three of them were weaving mats of *Vetiveria nigritana*, a swamp grass which grows to great heights all over Africa. The fishermen got theirs from a stand growing in a shallow depression beside the encampment. A number of waterholes had been dug there, and two Shuwa girls giggled when they discovered Waz and me washing off the morning's encrustations.

The camp itself was occupied by upwards of one hundred men dressed up as tramps. I doubt if they had a yard of unripped cloth between them. They were variously engaged in stringing hooks and mending gear or sleeping under the low grass shelters. The whole place looked like a feral beach club whose members had arranged a little bloater curing in the sands. Black pits the size of minivans winked up like blinded ogres, some half patched with greasy tin and others gummed by rows of fish laid out on wooden racks. In one hole fluffy worms of ash were settling to a powder. The pits were charged with bone dry grass and, once lit, flared quickly to char and smoke the fish. Bundles of firewood were stacked nearby to fuel more thorough smoking, but with wood so scarce the process was largely completed by further drying in the sun. The fish were nearly all of one species, namely *Clarias anguillaris*, a mud fish roughly twelve inches long which comprises about seventy-five per cent of the total Lake Chad catch. Clarias resemble streamlined tadpoles and they end up on the smoking pits like quoits, their tails jammed in their mouths on pointed bits of stick. They are sold in markets throughout the country and, having seen thousands of them on previous occasions, I neglected to ask why they were rolled up. It may have been to prevent the fish lying against each other and obstructing the smoke.

Another thing I neglected to do was to look at the lake. The water was only five minutes' walk away and we could see chaps walking back from the swampy reeds with wet gill nets and the enormous gourds they used as floats. I had all the time in the world and I didn't even bother just to stroll over and take a look. I think that I was getting a bit obsessed with moving south, although there were certain other attractions in the camp itself, Fatima Mohamman being the main one. She was a Shuwa from a nearby encampment and had come over to barter milk for fish, squatting patiently in the usual Bornu market pose behind a large, decorated calabash. A split-gourd ladle poked out beneath the matting cover on which she put the small change, fish and maize which she had received for her milk.

Fatima had most sexy hair, a blatant smile and wanton, roving eyes. She also had a nose ring and an open zip across her dress, like horizontal flies from which it all hung out. To say her breasts were firm and ripe would be to overstate the case. They deserved, I thought, long service medals from the Milk Marketing Board, but they appeared to satisfy the grasping baby on her hip. The husky crackle in her voice made up for her wrinkled mammaries and she was basically a very tasty lady. I fancied her like hell, but, needless to say, did nothing about it. In 1978 the dispensary at Mallam Fatori dealt with 200 cases of bilharziasis, 1,500 of conjunctivitis, 2,000 of malaria, but 2,400 of gonorrhoea and syphilis combined. In any case she probably didn't fancy me.

I suppose that tensions and strains existed in that fishing camp as they do in most isolated work places, but I was struck by the apparent peace and outward calm. Some of the men were fishing on their own account but the rest did not have the air of being simply hired flotsam. Their presence was justified by more than coin and labour. The European idea that an employer and an employee can be linked solely by money and the job in hand is, I think, foreign to traditional African systems. Values and attitudes are, of course, changing in Africa as well as in Europe and are constantly adapting to new circumstances, but, generally speaking, Africa is not yet reconciled to the somewhat one dimensional approach that Europeans have to their work relationships. The distinction between work and social life, generally so clear in Europe, is not so easy to draw in some other parts of the world. As a broad generalisation, having agreed on wages and conditions, ve in Europe now begin der work, ja? Not in Bornu. We now begin to be related, I, the patron with yet another follower in my household, and you, the client, benefiting from my status as a "big man", to which your clientship also makes its contribution. Many of the fishermen were clients of middle men based in Baga, Kukawa and other towns and they had attached themselves to the families and the fortunes of their patrons. This client-patron arrangement seemed to me to be typical of a fundamental difference between Europeans and Africans.

Europeans move in a world of things. They desire Objects, and they live as if experience were also a series of objects. They "have" marriages, jobs, houses, good days, bad days, and children. Africans, by contrast, are into power. They desire People, and although they pursue material riches with as much enthusiasm as do Europeans, they do so with far less attachment to the object itself than to its effect. Africans are into conspicuous consumption and appalling bad taste because the thing itself does not really matter. What does matter is the power that the object symbolises. It doesn't matter that a house might be a cess pit, windowless and rank. The man has had it built and it fills up with his people. See, there he goes in his robes and his Peugeot, a big man whose power can rub off on me. The robes and cars are flags round which his people rally. They are not yet, as in Europe, bricks in a wall which can rise so alarmingly, dividing us each one a hermit in our opulence.

I first arrived in Nigeria as a freshly unwrapped graduate with a reasonably clear idea that people would be playing a different cultural game to the one that I had left behind. Accepting that such cultural differences existed was no problem, but handling the day-to-day manifestations of the differences was another thing altogether. I did not know the rules, far less the extent to which they could be broken, bent or simply ignored. While fully prepared to adapt my hitherto European assumptions, I could not judge the extent to which what I did was right, acceptable or reasonable, nor could I tell when I was simply being taken for a ride. I was nonplussed, for example, at the continuing and, I thought, undignified stream of petty requests from a man I first employed as a cook. He was seventy, a grandfather several times over and had worked in some pretty grand households. Here was this venerable old boy now in the employ of a young sproat and begging favours like a child, favours that he didn't need anyway. I was embarrassed, confused and sometimes annoyed at this constant importunity, until I woke up to the fact that this man was not so much an employee as a dependant. I was his "big man" and by judicious accession to his requests I could enhance my own status as well as contributing to his coffers or his larder. One was never actually asked to give anything directly. It was always, "This man say make you help him with small, small . . ." whatever it was he wanted. I was, of course, ripped off mercilessly, but I felt more comfortable about being bamboozled once I had discarded my precise notions of how things should be. I began to live within slightly different limits, but it took a long time for me to appreciate just how deeply ingrained was my "Europeanness" and how inflexible were my patterns of thought.

Wandering about the fishing camp I noticed that a standing man was about the most substantial thing upon the landscape.

A petty trader had set up shop, a kaleidoscope of necessaries stacked under the woven shade of his shelter, and arranged with the minute attention that produces bottled ships and models made of matchsticks. A jailed head gardener might have planted out the sundries on the traders' little table. The brand names were a lecture on the state of trade—imperial twitches from Lipton's tea and tubes of Trebor mints, cooking oil and kola nuts from the agricultural present, chewing gum, soap and Jet, the Extra Strong Detergent, perhaps forerunners of an industrial future. Three Rings, the worst fags in the world, were blooming in a garden of cheap batteries and penny tins of Robb, a universal unguent made, I suspect, from dead koala bears. To accompany the cigarettes were boxes of microcephalic matches which, when struck, would behead themselves and sail up one's shorts like smoking lice.

We continued over the treeless burnt-off surface. Green shoots were already poking up from cauterised tufts of grass, and away towards the east a tousled screen of papyrus waved in drowning silhouette. Although the lake was creeping forward on its annual dispersion, there were no signs of anything remotely damp. The water could have been a thousand miles away.

Two riders overtook us, sitting deep between their high Bornu cantels and saddle horns of Viking elegance. Long bags of maize hung down across the ponies' withers, half sheltering the slippered feet which in their coloured espadrilles weighed flat on shovel bladed stirrups. The horsemen drew away and left us to the sun. Ahead and off the track a long black stick was shimmering, precise and dark, too solid for a shadow. It quivered then and, like a satin javelin, it slid across the path. Claude had seen Egyptian cobras before and remained unimpressed, except to stutter forward at an even slower pace. We excused him on the grounds of his curly feet. We had them trimmed that very night in the village of Dawartsin Hausari. An operative with a mallet and a sharpened bolt cut off the excess horn and gave our Claude some hay, which he ignored.

He fell instead and rather greedily upon the hut in which we spent the night.

The headman sent two little girls with rice and milk for our breakfast. They put down their trays and waited while we ate. Waz was feeling sorry for Claude.

"He had an awful night," said Waz. "Gar! Every time he was bitten he went 'Hnnnn' and shook all over. I couldn't get to sleep."

After such a night poor Claude was not on form. He wiggled in his tortoiseshell of gear, and mincing forward took the high road like an outcast, burdened by a carapace of sin. Jalo did the driving, a frustrating task since slowing to the donkey's awkward pace required a certain concentration. There had been no trees in sight for two days now and, in lieu of a cane, Jalo swished a futile piece of rope.

"Cla-orrd," he said, clicking his teeth for the first syllable. He sounded like a frog in trouble. "Cla-orrrd!" About a week later we discovered that he assumed the word "Claude" was the English for "donkey". That day, however, he gave Claude a surname. "Mr. No-road", he called him, adding certain less savoury titles as the day progressed.

"Cla-orrd Bahanya," we heard him muttering towards midday. "Claude Bahanya dan shege dan gogo." Translated from the Hausa these are abusive words, actionable in Muslim courts. As conferred by Jalo, Claude's full title was "Cla-orrd No-road, Son of a Bastard, Seed of Baboon", but the "Seed of Baboon" was a words-will-never-hurt-me sort of chap who retaliated by turning the other cheek. He turned it so often and with such maddening persistence that one of us eventually had to lead him by a rope. He would pitch off into the surrounding bush like a fly-half on the break and seemed incapable of advancing south directly. I came to the conclusion that he was a bit of a subversive.

The afternoon droned on. Hearing Jalo's voice, I turned. He was in earnest conversation with a stand of sugar cane which told him in Kanuri just to help himself. A piping treble rustled through the plot. It emerged to take our cash and its name was

100

Usman Ibrahim. From Usman's sticky fingers dangled half a dozen locusts, strung together with the boyish skill that preserves eggs uncracked on descents from tall trees and keeps captured lizards ticking in the flotsam of a trouser pocket. Usman Ibrahim was not, however, a natural historian, but a hungry boy and the locusts were for his lunch. We did not join him but tore into the sugar cane, which is such satisfying stuff to eat. You can scratch your back with it or use it as a walking stick and it makes a super noise inside your head with all the scrunching going on between your teeth. The fibrous outer skin rips off in strips as working down from node to node you grind up mouthfuls of the pith, suck it dry and spit it out in a private snowstorm. The last few inches of cane are always tricky to hold, and I just threw my stump at the deviating Cla-orrd. He didn't care.

The sky that day was dilute blue, the land quite pale and flat, and the only colour in the world came from cattle egrets bold against the grass. The egrets rose like agitated handkerchiefs, and, pulling away regretfully, they flapped towards a drooling herd whose dottle joggled brightly in the sun. The secretions and the linen rush were, we realised, in favour of a shallow glint which we could see now. The lake was on its way, no deeper than your toes, but creeping forward like a lukewarm bath, magical in discontinuity and instant in effect; the earth was either dry and brown, or black, submerged and wet. Scummy dollops twizzled at the very edge where surface tension played elastic, teasing games with the detritus of the season. Shrivelled leaves and broken corn stalks bobbed away like transports with unwilling insect crews, and beetles, taken up, were turning like loose oil drums upon the sudden ocean. A wriggling vanguard of small fry was flowing past already, with tadpoles, small green frogs and tiny fish. The thirsty cows splashed in and kicked their own reflections.

Beyond the water was another Hausa village where we rested. An evacuation was under way. Carts and pick-ups were being stacked with house poles, mats and varied chattels, and, like uncovered wagons, they were heading west. Our own way ahead was cut, and so that afternoon we made a wide detour across a plain with nothing but the blue above and lightish green below. A man with awful smallpox marks drove by with a canoe tied on his Datsun. It overhung the cab, on which I climbed to get a wider view, but all I saw was much more of the same wide watercolour. The Datsun itself was loo-tile yellow. At tea time we reached an Uda camp. Waz took photographs, including one of a young Uda woman giving me a maize cob. In handing me this prize she made the observation that I was evidently incapable of growing maize myself—my hands were far too soft, which was odd, she said, since I had a beard and was clearly well past boyhood.

"Maize for an old man," the Uda woman said, "maize for an old man from an old lady." She was only about twenty-five herself, but, indicating Waz, she smiled. "Why is your brother taking pictures of old grandparents?" she said. Without Waz to translate, the pleasant banter of the wayside would have been replaced by formal and boring intercourse of the "Me Tarzan, you Jane" variety, with uneasy bonhomie that I was happy to avoid.

Long applause of distant smoke rolled in scalloped tiers across the sun. Slick, boomerang shaped swifts and swallows like barbed arrowheads were dancing death to insects on the wing, while more white egrets, crook necked and tumbledried, flapped overhead. A blunt faced harrier chopped sleek and silver just above the grass unnerving its supper to break cover. We saw specimens of this bird nearly every day until we reached the mountains. They were, I think, Pale harriers, although they could have been adult male Montague's harriers which are also grey. Apart from well known migrants like cuckoos, swallows and nightingales, a very large number of other European birds spend the winter south of the Sahara.

The trickle and the crackling of burning grass came on across the empty plain and wisps of cirrus, reinforced by smoke, banked as an evening mist against the sun. Like the tiny ants with which we shared the track we moved on across unbroken distances towards the point at which all parallels converge, until, at just that point, a loveliness emerged which stopped us dead. It seemed as if a matador had twirled a net of thistledown or lace into the sky, each knot an individual life, the whole controlled so perfectly not one bird broke the ranks. The flock billowed gigantically, a wave which had at last leapt free of the confining ocean. It sank to the ground and whirled again, describing arcs and curves of superb complexity, now expanding, now clustering tight, shifting constantly its density, now shrunk to a bee-black cloud, now bursting out once more to lace and thistledown. The flow of birds appeared to wrap the sky and then it disappeared, attenuated, to magic out upon a screen of evening air in effects mathematical. There were millions and millions of them. They looked a bit like common sandpipers, but were actually ruffs, birds which live in swamps and marshy places. I do not quite know why they dance but it has been suggested that they are conducting a census among themselves.

And so we reached a small maize farm where a man and his two wives were almost finished with their agricultural labours for the year. They were bagging up the grain, but had stopped work for the night. We ate rice and pappy macaroni with sardines, onions and tomato paste and Claude had a delicious roll just as the stars came out. We were packed and off before the sun appeared and when it did it dribbled up insipid as the yolk from factory eggs. The beehive huts of a Fulani camp cast faint shadows through the cool dawn air, and placid cows were parked at random over some dozen moist, green acres. The grass was, however, alive with grounded ruffs, pecking at the dung pats and the hoof marks like hyper-active lepre-chauns. Following the sunset show I was not surprised to see their pressing appetites.

I spent most of that day's rest time ogling the Shuwa women who wandered past the shelter we had occupied. The Shuwas are more recent arrivals on the Bornu scene than the Kanuris, who have evolved in situ, but, like the Kanuri ancestors, the Shuwas came originally from the Yemen. Their language is a dialect of Arabic and they tend to have pale skins and straightish hair. Most Shuwa families lead varied lives, mixing pastoralism with farming in a flexible economy that more or less depends upon the level of Lake Chad.

In gaps between the Shuwas I observed a fellow hut guest crawling round the matting wall at speeds so low that even Claude looked fast. I find chameleons spellbinding, but Waz didn't like them much and Jalo thought them poisonous. The Kanuris say that chameleons move in their ponderous and deliberate way because the earth was still soft when God made them.

Preparing for the afternoon's physicals I collected Claude from his usual hut munching and noticed that he looked even less bright eyed than normal. While loading him I found the cause of his discontent. Something had done a Merchant of Venice job on his neck, which, though not bleeding, was missing rather more than just one pound of flesh. He had obviously been attacked by a demented beaver. I cleaned the wound and, as we moved off, we caught sight of another donkey smirking round the back of a hut. It too had a lump on its neck, but not as big or raw as Claude's. Our boy had obviously got the worst of a fight and I felt humiliated. Chatting as we went, Jalo, Waz and I decided that our lad needed help, and we determined therefore to buy him a friend.

At about five o'clock we sighted our first trees for three days and when we came to one in which a tawny eagle sat we stopped and made our camp. Waz and Jalo set up the nets while I cut hay for Claude, giving myself a blood blister in the process. The Uda lady had been right about my hands but at least my feet were hardening up. There were no jolly songs around the camp fire that night. Supper was a three man game of pass the parcel, the forfeit being a severe mauling from the mosquitoes if you were caught outside your net. I burnt large holes in mine by knocking the mosquito coil over in my sleep and woke up feeling lots of sympathy for whoever it was had died last at the Alamo.

The trees were a welcome contrast to the days of openness behind us. Although there were still plenty of acacias, the trees were generally less spiny than they had been further north, and some of them were pretty big. We saw a few large bombaxes with buttressed trunks, their bright red flowers still in bud. Being exceptionally useful, the tamarinds and baobabs had been allowed to remain on land cleared for farms and rose with the isolated dignity of park dwellers. The average level of tree growth was, however, still fairly modest, with extensive breaks of bare *Lannea humilis* which I called joker trees. They reminded me of the writhing growths which appear behind the jokers in some packs of cards. The prettiest tree in this lower region of the lake was Anogeissus leiocarpus with its weeping habit and its slightly zigzag twigs, a northern representative of the family Combretaceae that we were to see more of in the Guinea savannahs further south. The most useful new plant for us was a humble shrub which grew abundantly on abandoned farm land. Its real name was Guiera senegalensis, but I called it donkey-go bush. A switch of guiera raised Claude's octane rating instantly and he would scuttle forward at the very sound of the right bush being broken off. We were still keen to recruit a running mate for him and that afternoon we stopped at a village called Baderi to make enquiries.

Although there were no taps, Baderi was supplied with a system of stand pipes which gushed fizzy Artesian water into stagnant pools. I sat in the mud and let the glorious onslaught shower through my hair. Jalo only took a little sip and disappeared, but I anchored Claude while Waz also soaked himself. Jalo came back. He had found a man of unpleasant countenance (almost a twin of Claude's previous owner) who was willing to sell a donkey. He too was demanding a ridiculous sum. The dark coloured animal before us was a younger, sleeker beast than Claude, but less well endowed. We bought him, and, for no special reason, called him Norman.

As predicted four weeks earlier, there were Greeks in the bush. We spotted our first one that afternoon. He trundled slowly by in his Land-Rover, with an air gun poking out of the window. He stopped every so often to whang off a pellet, a pathetic and peculiarly south European sight. The man must have turned sixteen stone, and he looked ridiculous as he retrieved a vinaceous dove which was far too small to eat. He made me feel ashamed.

The earth round Kirinawa had been stripped bare and stroked with large machines. Stencilled crates were stacked in rows like city blocks and we passed incongruously between them, coming eventually to a chainlink fence containing bungalows and shady trees. Four hundred Greeks had occupied the compound through the late seventies as work had progressed on the South Chad Irrigation Project, a scheme designed to bring water from the south pool of the lake to a huge area of canalised bush. A pumping station was presently being constructed by a German company. Like a gigantic heart, the pumps would lift the water through about two metres and pour it into an arterial system which was to irrigate thousands and thousands of acres. The pumps were capable of delivering a greater flow of water than the Thames at London Bridge, and we could already see the straight, clean lines of the new canal which had been cut to receive it. Most of the Greeks had left, but Nick, the camp boss, was still there. He presented us with an air conditioned cabin each. What blessings are electricity and beds and water from a tap.

Despite the irrigation project, Kirinawa itself was a one hoss place. There were no yams or sweet potatoes for sale, and what particularly cheesed me off was the lack of gerin rogo, a preparation of grated cassava which looks and tastes like sawdust. It is one of the few instant Nigerian foods. All you do is add sugar and water, work up an undiscriminating appetite, and eat it. I managed to get some rice which was mostly gravel and weevils, and we stocked up on the inevitable tins of sardines and pilchards.

While Jalo prostrated himself before his air conditioner, Waz and I strolled across the compound to talk to Christine Betterton. She was a biologist, at work on some platyhelminths of the family Schistosomatidae. Platyhelminths are rather sordid manifestations of the Almighty's hand. They include among their ranks the tapeworm and the bloodfluke. Bloodflukes are nasty little creeps. They are hermaphrodites for a start, and they probably have spats and centre partings too.

Christine explained that bloodflukes kick off in the usual way as eggs and hatch into fresh water as hirsute blobs called miracidia. For some reason miracidia are partial to certain types of snails and they head straight up the shells of the nearest ones they can find. These are not your garlic studded escargot, but puny little freshwater jobs which lurk around the tropics and especially favour irrigation schemes. The miracidia bore into their hosts and undergo profound restructuring to emerge as free swimming larvae known as cercariae. A cercaria can splash about on its own for a day or two but unless it can find a human bod to burrow into, it dies. If its mining operations are successful, the cercaria heads for the blood vessels of the bladder and the intestine, drinking itself silly and laying eggs which work their way into the liver and the walls of other organs. Ironically it is the body's own immune response to the presence of the eggs that eventually shows itself as the disease bilharzia. Local inflammation leads to fibrosis and haemorrhage and, while not actually dying, the human host suffers severe debilitation. Bilharzia is easily man's most widespread parasitic disease and, unlike malaria, that other great parasitic scourge, bilharzia is on the increase. Christine's main concern was that the canal system should be kept free of weeds. Without grazing there would be no snails and without snails, no bloodflukes.

10

The Germans on the pumping station hardly glanced up from their welding as we straggled by beneath them. They wore bright denim cut-offs to a man and had fat legs.

From Kirinawa we were making a detour east to Gambaru where Waz's brother lived. We crackled on across the sun dried, cattle rutted bush. The stiff thorn was relieved occasionally by wet, green swamps where hammerkop and ibis fed under the scrutiny of slim grey herons. A Peugeot overtook us, stopped, reversed and spoke. Its number plate was BO 474 MB.

"Do you lack money to travel by car?" it asked. "But you are a European and you get reason, isn't it?"

"Mm," I said.

Later we passed an Uda camp hidden among the trees.

"How about staying with them?" I suggested. "Ask if they've got any milk and chat them up a bit." Waz looked unkeen, and wandered over half heartedly. He and Jalo preferred to stay in villages for the night but I liked to sleep in cattle camps or simply to crash out in the bush.

"They've got no milk and they say there's a village just up the road," said Waz. "Just up the road" turned out to be another two hours' walk. Perhaps the Fulanis didn't want us, I thought, or perhaps Waz didn't ask. Hairline cracks were opening along predestined lines. The heat would find them out. Lie back, I told myself, and don't be quite so brittle. I was trying to relax and curb my inclination to hurtle southward blinkered and oblivious to all but the final destination. We had months and months ahead of us and there really was no rush, my only genuine worry being that my money might run out.

We continued in silence through the gathering evening. Bits of track kept leaping up to heaven as nightjars in their camouflage took off beneath our feet. The males had lollipop shaped feathers trailing from each wing tip and presented crazy silhouettes against the sky. We arrived "just up the road" well after nightfall, and I woke up the following morning feeling grumpy.

We took the road to Gambaru under a sparse fleece of cirrus cloud, following a natural feature that I could at last distinguish. It was a degraded but still discernible remnant of the lake called the Ngalewa Ridge, an ancient shore line cut some fifteen miles short of Gambaru by the Mbuli river. I should add that, as far as the Mbuli is concerned, images of trout and kingfishers are misplaced, and thoughts of wild, white water are quite inappropriate. Think rather of a concrete desolation, for the Mbuli is the colour and consistency of wet cement. When we arrived it had ceased to move and was congealing round the spiny undergrowth. It had little else to do but linger in the sun, evaporate and obstruct communications. I waded across to check the depth while the others unloaded the donkeys. The village of Wurge rose from the far bank. It looked much like the river, being also grey and earthy. The younger villagers were curious and lined the bank as we edged Norman towards the low drop. In fact it was Norman who was doing the edging as I discovered when he flicked me into the water with a slurp. I emerged plastered in all the Mbuli had to offer, and I looked like a recently discovered tribe. Flailing towards the survivors of what I could already picture as the Great Mbuli River Disaster I began to swear, and must have put the wind up Norman, because at the sight of me he took off across the river like a sea slug in a rush.

Meanwhile I had asked Waz to make a photographic record of Jalo, Claude and me in transit. Between the grunts and snorts I was aware of clicks at what I judged to be wrong moments. Being short of film I was annoyed, unreasonably, since I was not at the viewfinder and, as it turned out, Waz's pictures were actually rather good. We were getting on top of one another and at midday I lay panting in a flimsy scrap of shade wondering what to do about it. Norman looked fed-up as well. He stood inert and miserable in a thicket.

Jalo asked me for a needle. I supposed that he had a splinter.

"No," he said, as I handed over a shiny new one from the darning kit. "That's too small. I need a big one."

I wondered if he were suicidal. It was frightfully hot and I had got to a bit in *I Claudius* where people were trampolining about on their sword points. I gave Jalo my sailmaker's needle and, following him, we approached Norman's thicket. It was evidently the donkey who had the splinter.

"No problems, Norm," I said, "soon be better. That needle could dig out a cannon ball." Under Jalo's directions I got Norman in a headlock and jammed a stick into his mouth. Jalo then stabbed him sharply in the palate.

"Ahh!" I said.

Norman said nothing. He must have been speechless with shock. Jalo's next move was to give the roof of Norman's mouth a vigorous scraping. The idea was to let a little blood. It would do Norman the world of good, said Jalo, wiping off the needle.

As we returned to our mats several dozen cows filtered across the track, followed by two Shuwa herdsmen. One of them stopped to pass the time of day with Jalo. By their gestures I could see that they were talking about Norman. The Shuwa, whose name was Hassan, drew his knife and, with Norman again in a headlock, he re-operated. He massaged Norman's nose, inducing a few reluctant drops of blood to fall on to the sand. I could hardly bear it and Waz had turned quite pale, but if the Shuwas did it to their own animals I supposed it was all right. The treatment seemed more like grievous bodily harm than veterinary science.

Hassan passed on the cheerful news that a gang of Fulanis from Chad had cut the throat of a Shuwa herdsman the day before and had shot another as he escaped across the Mbuli, close by the ford we had just used. The gang had been terror-ising the district. Their operational procedure was to attack

110

either at the dead of night or at midday when everybody was asleep. Prodding Norman into action we hurriedly left, hoping to reach Gambaru that night. We did not.

"Norman's getting worse," said Waz.

"Not surprising really," I said, and at the same time had a brilliant idea. "Why don't you go ahead and find your brother, then come out and meet us in the morning?"

"OK," said Waz. Bornu townsfolk are relatively easy to find, since anonymity is not part of the local urban scene. Waz would just ask the first Marghi that he saw, or, failing that, he would look for the meat chief. Waz's brother was in the meat trade and would certainly be known to the headman of the Gambaru butchers.

Jalo and I, meanwhile, turned off the track and picked our way between thorn fences and the huts of a Shuwa village called Shankoriya. From the air a Shuwa village looks like a cluster of old compost heaps. The huts are more like byres than the usual neat rondavels, and but for the roof props there is room inside most of them to swing a very long tailed cat. The roofs themselves are shaped like hairy mushrooms, the tousled thatching being ruffled punk in style. One felt like leaping on it with an enormous comb.

A man called Hamid was sitting cross-legged beneath a tamarind. In respect for his age we called him Baba which means "father". On the mat beside him was a kettle. In West Africa kettles are a sign of prayer—just ordinary, cheap old kettles, used daily by millions of people to pour water for their ritual ablutions before praying. Most taxis and lorries have one aboard somewhere and there is usually at least one in every compound.

Baba Hamid's rosary clicked steadily through his fingers. He cocked a wrinkled eye and sucked his teeth as Jalo explained our presence. The sun bounced off his pate, throwing a shadow from the veins which wriggled up his temples as he replied. At his invitation we dumped the gear on mats provided by his grandchildren and we hobbled both the donkeys.

If the Shuwas were surprised by our arrival they did not

111

show it. In fact they behaved rather as if we were expected. The same could not be said of the nearby Kanuri settlement from whose borehole the Shuwas took their water. Jalo and I went to bathe and between a preliminary splash and a final rinse I counted thirty-seven people who turned up to gawp in the street-corner curiosity one had gradually learnt to ignore. Shankoriya was, of course, much smaller than its Kanuri neighbour, being occupied only by Baba Hamid, his sons, and their families, some of whom were absent on their farms near the lake.

As the sun diminished, calves and yearlings tripped into the byres, and the thorn enclosures filled with mature beasts led in from the surrounding plain. The muted "pud pud" of dung falling in the dust died as the herd settled for the night. Lamps were lit and the orange glow of insufficient kerosene threw the shadows of twisted roof poles over milk cows tethered with their calves. Sleeping platforms, raised off the accumulating floor of each byre, were strewn with hard pillows stuffed with kapok from a bombax tree. The Shuwas lived in the closest possible contact with their animals.

It is, perhaps, a poor reflection on my character, but without an English-speaking companion I felt light and free that night. Waz's absence allowed me to slip a cultural clutch, to disengage and coast along in neutral for a while. Whatever the subject, each communication with him was like a journey back to England, and, while I could never entirely escape my background, his presence tended to reinforce it. Without him I was isolated and could assume a partial anonymity. I was not obliged to participate in my own culture since, without speech, I was passively rather than actively foreign. I was reminded of the well known Buddhist poser about the sound of one hand clapping. Perhaps one hand can make a noise, but, without another, the noise is not very loud. I also realised that I had been, in truth, walking on my own. Waz just happened to be there and I was, in a certain sense, treating him as an interruption and not as a contribution. Despite my intentions of sharing the experience of the walk I was not doing so.

First steps, me following Jalo.

First camp: Jalo and I making tea, Mallam Baida.

The lake creeping up on Waz.

Shua herd.

Kanuri girl selling milk. Her necklace is of silver Maria Theresa dollars.

Three sisters—Kanuri girls warming themselves at dawn.

Trouble with the donkeys: Jalo, Norman and I in the River Mbuli.

Waz and Claude on the Guduf tr

An old Waa clansman.

The Maiden of the Mandaras.

Fatima of the fish camp.

The Rockosaurs from Futude cemetery.

A headload of sorghum
approaching Ngossi.

Traditional Vomengu dress—
Dlimo's wife near Visik.

orence Nightingale strikes again.

Waz unpacking in Arnado's
compound near Potokov river.

Borroro youth near the Benue.

Borroro woman in Gwoza.

Young Borroro girl.

Wafundumta's wife:
Marghi facial marks.

Crossing the Benue, Waz seated, Michel standing in canoe.

Although I have relished the solution of physical problems, I have always found personal ones easy to walk away from. In travelling without companions of a similar culture one avoids the constant self-adjustments necessary to retain harmony, and one's journeys can become periods of literal self-indulgence. As such they can be unhealthy and unchallenging. But, despite one's feeble attempts to live less selfishly, the realisation is not the deed. I was finding it difficult to accommodate to the presence of a companion and I wondered how far Waz would come.

I was able to converse with the Shankoriya people because most of them spoke some Hausa. Drinking long calabashes of milk, Jalo and I listened in the darkness to a tale of woe from Baba Hamid. Part of his herd was across the border in Chad and in the present warlike situation he feared for its safety. Worse, a son of his was languishing in jail. The son had caught a lone Fulani in the act of milking off the Shankoriya herd. Assuming the Fulani to be a rustler, the son had promptly shot him with his bow and marched him to the nearby police post at Ngala. There, to his immense surprise, he had been detained.

"That's Nigeria today," said Baba Hamid. "By God! You can't even shoot someone without being arrested."

The village dogs became hysterical during the small hours. Jalo woke me up, muttering something about hyenas, and so I fumbled for the torch and staggered about the byres looking for Claude and Norman. I found them beyond the village and drove them into a corral where they became honorary cows for the rest of the night. At just about the time that I was settling back to sleep Ronald Reagan was elected President of the United States. Waz had been looking forward to hearing the radio reports and when we met up again the following morning he told us all about it. He had managed to find his brother, whose name was Teku, and we were expected.

Waz had arrived at an opportune moment. We were in the middle of an enormous open field system which had been bulldozed from the bush ten years earlier to form the pilot scheme for the Lake Chad Irrigation Project. The irrigation ditches were crossed by substantial concrete bridges over which the donkeys would not go. Claude had just performed his Houdini act and Norman had simply folded. His legs had slithered like dividers on a globe and he had hit the dust. We were not strong enough to pick him up and I did not relish the more drastic remedy of lighting a fire underneath him as suggested by Jalo. Waz's patience eventually won the day. He gently draped his khaki shirt over Claude's reluctant head and led him like a blinded Turk across the bridge. Norman got up and followed.

The bush beyond the fields lay broken by the ceaseless clack of hooves converging on the high road. Cattle driven through from the Cameroons and Chad had ground the land near Gambaru to dust.

Ignoring national boundaries, cattle dealers and their agents scour the hinterland, buying up an odd cow here or there, and they gradually assemble big mobs to be driven, or, more precisely, led, down to Maiduguri. The capital of Bornu is a railhead and an entrepôt, the African equivalent of Santa Fe or Denver where, loaded into trucks, the beasts go south for slaughter. The cowboys are almost all Fulanis, dusty from the trail, their heads wound round in indigo, their hands draped gracefully on the staves they hitch across their shoulders. They gangle on, loose limbed, between the sunrise and the sunset, a grimy plastic bottle sloshing gently from a string or, perhaps, a kettle in their hands. Their gear is nothing more than mats, pots and sacks of flour and it travels on a bull.

We crawled on against the flow of cows. Soft rubber sighs whooshed by as cars bowled down the tarmac into shimmering obscurity. The vehicles materialised and faded off like something out of *Star Wars*, emanations from the town which now we had on visual, a blip near the horizon. The sun and dust made distances deceptive, obscuring the cables of a communications mast ascending into heaven from the Cameroonian post of Fotokol. Gambaru, on the Nigerian side, was largely made of unfired earthenware and seemed to be awaiting patiently its turn in the celestial kiln. The town was roughly ten feet high and half a mile across, its walls and streets all beaten earth, but for the single tarmac road and desultory stabs at public drainage. The open ditches had been bridged by infrequent paving stones and, in places, spun concrete pipes were stacked, no doubt with good intentions. We stayed two nights.

Waz's brother lived just off the maidan, an area the size of two dry football fields. In the evenings it filled with wobbly Honda-men. Some wore robes and others jeans but they all rode in unsteady circuits just like Sammy Seals, round and round the dusty square. Their instructors sat on battered oil drums. Small boys, of course, looked on with desirous fantasy, or dashed about with rags to polish up the shiny bits when novices fell off. Rags were also tied in bundles for casual games of barefoot kickabout while livestock sauntered into town from the day's grazing. Goats dallied over anything organic, snorting at bits of cardboard, trash and orange peel and hopping up the midden heaps. At dawn the herdboys called from compound to compound, collecting up the animals again to take them out to graze. The cow in Waz's brother's house did not go out because she was about to calve.

Waz had led us to a tin door set in a blank mud wall. We had unloaded the donkeys and had coaxed them over the threshold, through a narrow chamber where a chap was busy ironing, and out into a sunlit courtyard. Nigerian irons are large brass-bound affairs, quaint as the age of steam and they run on glowing charcoal. They require careful handling. Eight small rooms faced each other in two blocks of four across the yard. An awning of mats was raised in dappled compromise between the dark rooms and the open heat, and backing on to the whole area were higher walls of the surrounding buildings. Each room housed a family which worked out overall at about two full rugby teams residing in a squash court, with, as I have mentioned, a somewhat pregnant cow. Into this space came

115

Waz and I with both our donkeys, all our gear, and Jalo who did not stay long. We said goodbye, I paid him off and gave him a mosquito net. He changed from shorts and smock into his robe and matching trousers, and, with the floppy suitcase in his hand, he slipped off into town.

Waz and Teku were full brothers, "same mother, same father" as the usual qualification went. They looked alike. Despite their very different educations their relationship seemed easy and without strain. Teku means "ocean" in Hausa but I forgot to ask how he had acquired this nickname. Teku only had one wife, a heavily pregnant girl of seventeen. His neighbours were also young marrieds, each family paying about twenty pounds a month in rent. This may not sound much but in Teku's case it was roughly half his income. He had vacated his room for Waz and me and would sleep in a neighbouring compound.

There were a couple of rooms at the end of the yard which were used as kitchens where the women all cooked together. Most of them were Marghis. I watched them through the heat of the day, splintering large hunks of wood with the small axes of West Africa, bringing in pails of water on their heads and shooing off the chickens. In the evening croo–crooing doves flew down and strutted on the flat roof of the bog, a lean-to with a concrete floor laid across a deep, dark hole. The lean-to was where everybody washed as well, each with a loofah of palm fibres, another humble but universal detail of daily life in West Africa.

Teku had been given a start in the meat business by a senior relative. Butchering did not involve the permanent occupation of premises, nor a regular service to the public, but Teku was established with a right to a place in the market and he was recognised by the other butchers. The climate is against anything like a steady supply of meat through the day, and so butchers' shops tend to be set up in the cool of dawn and last only as long as it takes to dismember a carcass and sell it. Teku said that the key to success was in judging how much meat was on a cow before you bought it. Without the benefit of a weighbridge this was a difficult estimation to make and depended on an experienced eye. Having bought their animal, Teku and his colleagues usually paid a mallam to cut its throat with a prayer, and then they reduced it to small lumps as fast as possible, working against the sun and the flies. Other stall holders would crowd round and put in bids, and, with luck, the carcass would be sold within three hours. Teku made stuff called kilishi with the leftover meat. Kilishi is a kind of savoury biltong. The meat is beaten paper thin, then dried, and a mixture of spices is rubbed over it. It tastes absolutely gorgeous but is expensive.

We had come to the market early, but people were already breaking open sacks of oranges and spilling them into large tin baths of water. Young men with rolled-up trouser legs were washing the oranges with detergent, while merchants looked on and supervised the loading of an infant sales force, ready and waiting with its trays and razor blades. The purchase of an orange in Bornu includes a free peeling service.

I spent a good deal of my time in Gambaru at rest. So did Norman and Claude. They were fed a medicine of guinea corn and tobacco dust but they continued with their brazen lust for matting. I lay within hitting range and every time Claude's nose drew nigh I punched it through the mat. He didn't really get the message, and probably thought that the grass wall was trying to jump into his mouth. A chameleon absorbed me for an afternoon, performing impossible feats of yoga with its back legs and its tail, and I was fortunate enough to meet the local metallurgists.

On the far side of the maidan was a crumbling hut where the metallurgists were based, and against the walls were stacks of shiny cauldrons, winking in the sun like aluminium skulls. The production team was in action on the floor—not a great deal of action since the head had just come off their only decent hammer. The moulding process left certain imperfections which needed to be smoothed off or to be stopped up, and some of the pots, or marmites as they were called, looked more like sieves. The really bad ones were broken up and thrown on to a pile of engine casings and cracked manifolds awaiting melt down in the corner. The men were Bambaras by tribe and a cheerful lot, originally from Mali. They had been living in Chad for the past seven years but recent disturbed circumstances had precipitated their departure, as one of them put it. I stuck my head in through the window and leant on the sill for a chat.

"Bonjour," I said.

"Merrcii," said they, rolling their "r"s like barrels on a cobbled hill. I fell head-over-heels for their French. A lady was squatting in the doorway with a red purse in her lap. She had evidently been there for some time.

"Touta l'aprrès midi," said one of the Bambaras. His name was N'Djie. "Touta l'aprrès midi et touta la nuit, demain, aprrès demain comprenez vous-toujourrrs—le prix est fixé, ETERRNEL, et ne changerra jamais." The woman said nothing. She counted up the notes and the small change in her hand and pretended not to have understood. An hour or so went past. The Bambaras tinkered on, smoked all my cigarettes and talked. The woman was ignored. She had been quibbling over farthings for the past five hours and the pot she wanted had long since been put back on the stack. She finally stood up and sauntered away to a chorus of dumb cheers and smirks all round.

"Touta l'aprrès midi de perrdu pour des cacahuètes," said N'Djie. "Ça c'est la femme." I departed on a tide of fraternal understanding and returned the following day for a tour of the works. The pots were a copy of a well known French make and came in three sizes.

"Alorrs, les marmites," said N'Djie. He interrupted himself with a few personal details. His father was the ex-post master of Bamako, "actuellement parrti pour la retraite," but, if I should ever be in Bamako, N'Djie urged me to "Demande a l'ancien chef des postes." I wondered whether retired functionaries of the Malian postal service had a Saharan equivalent of Bexhill-on-Sea. N'Djie's pater however was living out his golden years in the capital where he had worked. We returned to the commentary which was intensely detailed and touchingly personalised.

"When the hammer has finished his work, the fire begins, the fire dies, he has completed his job. Now the file begins her task." N'Djie went from stage to stage. "On fait this, on mettre that, on renverse the other." It was like a televised recipe. "Maintenant le chapeau," he said as we got to the moulding process, "on tourn, son trravail est finis, enleve, et le voila!"

The tools were crude and portable. An air raid siren set into the floor blew a draught into the charcoal fire. The fan was geared to a cycle wheel that could have served on early Tours de France but which had since shed its pedals for two six-inch nails. The moulds were simple wooden trays to hold the dampened sand in place. If small is beautiful, the Bambara's operation was exquisite. By an odd coincidence I found myself in Bamako some six months later, but, needless to say, I did not bump into N'Djie's old dad.

11

Steam whispered pale but innocent from the morning cooking drums of waiting refugees. They stood in muted clusters and the orderly green tents hung still. The camp lay on the outskirts of the town and as we had approached it the pious muttered blessings. "God is King," they had said. "Allah ya Sarki." They had assumed that yet another pair of displaced Chadians was passing by, and they implied that God rules all of us, whatever our estate. Fortune, they were saying, lies in the hand of God. In English, I suppose, we would say, "Hard luck."

Another week went by beneath our feet. For three days we might have been becalmed upon a glassy ocean, for nothing broke the surface of the plain but faint irregularities. On the fourth day we saw a light, cigar-blue speck on the horizon and on the seventh we stood against the mountains. We had been walking for twenty-one days altogether and had covered between 250 and 300 miles since leaving Mallam Fatori. We weren't sure of the exact distance since our route had meandered over unmapped territory in a leisurely and not wholly accurate fashion. Anyhow, our plimsolls were finished.

The first fifty miles out of Gambaru was an extraordinary passage across an almost featureless plain. Waz summarised the landscape rather neatly.

"It's remarkable," he said, "there's so much sky."

The land was obviously liable to flood in the rains. Like coral islands scattered on the sea, low mounds were raised above the general uniformity, each one the location of a hamlet. Most of these sites were ancient. The archaeological excavation of Daima, a well formed mound just east of our route, has established a record of human occupation from 1000 B.C., and has turned up a succession of bone harpoons, clay figurines and artefacts in both iron and bronze.

For once our path was easy. We rolled south across the plains all day and at night we simply adjusted our course for the nearest mound, hoping that it was occupied. Some were not and these tended to be waterless. We spent the night of Waz's twentieth birthday on one of these empty tells, sipping tea among the silent baobabs and broken potsherds. Waz said that it gave him the creeps and cursed the lime juice in his radio. He missed the news, and savoured the last morsels of kilishi as consolation.

"Teku's kilishi is really good," said Waz," but you have to know who you buy it from—some people make it out of the worst bits of meat and old blankets."

"Blankets?"

"Yeah, they beat out old blankets and get them so thin that no one notices till they're through the spices and into the fluff."

"Good Lord!" I said.

That particular camp site was ant-ridden and several of them sank into my tea. One managed to recover as it floated past my incisors, and it bit me on the tongue, but I got my revenge. I swallowed it.

Despite the featureless landscape, our days were not without humour. We were stopped one day by a very long Shuwa who was reclining in the shade of a byre. He spoke pidgin English and hailed us as we straggled by. A wooden bowl of left-over guinea corn was thrust in our direction and, never willing to refuse a feed, we stopped. The guinea corn was terrible, being old, cold and dry, but the conversation more than compensated for our gastronomic discomfort. I wondered where our friend had learnt his pidgin.

"Dere for Lagos," he said. "Reach two year." Like many Shuwas, he had gone south and picked up casual work in the city. The open plains and the life of a cattleherd are perhaps not the best preparation for city life. Most of the migrant herdsmen tend to be employed as maigardis where their talent for sustained bouts of inactivity can be exploited to the full.

121

Our friend had not been a conspicuous success at even this undemanding work.

"I have particular," he said, digging a leather wallet from his robes. He extracted a grimy document, unfolding it with some reverence. He obviously thought that it said nice things about him. Here it is.

Fougerolle, Nigeria   25 Boyle St.,
                                                         7th Floor,
Pers/80/600/SE/ON   P.O. Box 5290,
                                                         Lagos.

Mallam Saula Abdulahi
12 Waziri Ibrahim Street
Victoria Island

Dear Sir,

Termination of appt.

In recent time your performance have fallen far below our desired need despite several advice to revive your effort.

As we can no longer condone your indulgence and abnormal attitude to work, quite evidenced, we have no alternative than to terminate your appt. at one month pay in lieu of notice. By a copy of this letter the Accounts dept. is advised to pay your wages to date and other entitlements accordingly.

We wish you future success,

Yours faithfully,
General Manager FN Ltd

Despite the wishes of the general manager, Abdulahi had not enjoyed future success and was back on the plains. The letter seemed an ironic bridge between two poles of existence.

It was still very hot. One's cigarettes were moistureless and smouldered at the gallop, while tea leaves dried up quickly if the cups were not swilled out. I thought of the November days

122

at home with cars slushing down the lanes and a big sea giving headaches to the ratepayers. Waz hummed "Johnny Come Marching Home" for a very long time, and we learnt a few words of Shuwa. Water was "alme" and walk was "almamsha". Rest was "t'nam", of which we required a great deal, but the most useful word was "darub" which meant path. Our darub was sometimes a convoluted affair. We became confused and highly disgruntled one day in what must have been the only swamp for hundreds of miles, and we were rescued by a chap on a horse. He was a local government messenger and he had a broad bladed spear which he waved. We followed him to a ford where he was kind enough to lend his weight to the hauling of Norman and Claude. The area was so damp that pink flowers like convolvulus carpeted the ground, and on the far side were gardens of tobacco plants and plots of late cereals, tripping through which came the Sisters of Mercy.

The horseman had continued on his way and Waz and I were reloading the donks, resigned to more paludal blunderings, when the sisters came swinging along by the water's edge. They were Shuwas, on the verge of plumpness, and wore identical dresses, homemade jobs, too tight above the waist and inelegant below, a sort of cast-off, mission design. One wore brass bangles between her elbows and her biceps and they both had nose rings and large calabashes on their heads. I think that they were returning from some far-off market.

We followed them after a good deal of sign language, taking a narrow path through grass tall enough to tickle a giraffe. The towering fronds reminded me of childhood when sometimes all the world is grown-ups' knees and shoelaces. Emerging on the open plains once more, I noticed that the President of the Ivory Coast was fluttering before us. The sisters had him in faded portrait flapping down their thighs. Many popular cloth designs in Africa commemorate the famous in this way. Elections and space shots are quite popular, as well as revolutions, although here the cloth designers have to read their morning papers carefully. The sisters were fairly typical in their choice of pattern. They stopped just short of the mound towards which we had been moving and they slipped into something more elegant for village wear. They put on wrappers, smothering President Houphouet Boigny with a surprising commemoration of the Silver Jubilee of our own dear Queen. Her Royal Highness bounced up the shallow rise into the hamlet with the letters E.R. 1977 scrolled in copper plate around her.

A dog and an old lady were sitting on the ground. The woman's hair hung in grey braids which looked odd against her skin. The sight of her out in the open suddenly made me realise what it was that gave Shuwa hamlets their free and open atmosphere—they had no matting screens around the huts like villages of other tribes. Although this fact was obvious it had taken me some time to become conscious of it. Bedding and belongings were rolled and lashed to the roofs in some of the Shuwa hamlets that we passed through, where the people had gone off in search of pasture. They would be back before the next year's rains to plant their farms again, but were able in the meantime to leave their homes unguarded.

We spent one night in a village where we learnt about the Pleiades. The Shuwa call this group of stars the "Elephant's Rump" and they call Orion's Belt the "Vulture". Our informant was 48122 Abu Dikwa, R.E. (retd.). He talked about his Commanding Officer, a Colonel Barlow, whom I did not know, and he asked for "Con Bif".

"What?" said Waz.

"Con Bif. Say you chop Con Bif make you dash me O?" said Abu Dikwa. Translated, this comes out as "Do you eat corned beef? If so please give me some." We offered a can of pilchards which Abu Dikwa accepted. He went on to tell us about the Suez Canal, Bombay, and Burma where he had served during the Second World War, apparently under a rain of corned beef parachuting from the sky. It was all a bit difficult to understand. For some reason Waz and I got talking about religion that night. Perhaps it was the stars. Open skies

124

and open landscapes do seem to produce reflective talk. The night wind was cool and wrapped in our sheets we watched our late night brew steaming on the fire. We fell silent, but I had drifted into certain other star-struck nights spent, not on the savannahs, but on the lolling sea.

12

Three years previously I had sailed for a month on board a small East African dhow or jahazi, sleeping on the open deck in the velvet murmur of the trades, and listening, through some of the nights, to the memories of a man called Ba Allen. He was then about eighty years old and I had helped him as I could. He established himself in the ship's dinghy, hauled up on the deck for the passage between Mombasa and Lamu, and from this modest cockpit he told me stories all the starry nights long.

Having been posted to Kenya as a frontier policeman soon after the First World War, he had stayed for the rest of his life, but Ba Allen was no retired colonial. He struck me as a cross between *Tom Brown's Schooldays* and *Sanders of the River*.

"Keep breaking bones," he said, "always have." He had a very shaky wrist. "Broke this arm about nine months ago. Fell through the hatch of this very dhow, bloody kuzini [a wind] blowing up the swell. Had a brigadier once, odd fellow, liked games. Used to get me and a boxing chap from another formation to fight in the mess. Always seemed to end up hitting the wall, kept breaking my wrists. Ha! Ha! Ha!" Ba Allen had an unbelievable laugh.

"My Swahili name's Bwana Kicheko," he said. "It means 'hollow, mocking laughter'. First person to call me that was an Arab girl in bed, ha ha ha!" His nickname in Masai was Tepetet. "That's a berry that the Morans take before they go fighting lions. It's a tapeworm medicine too. I suppose if you've got a tapeworm you wouldn't be much good at fighting lions, ha ha ha!" Needless to say, Kicheko had blue eyes, and

126

he had, of course, been speared in the course of duty. There was an enormous scar through his right elbow.

"Took one here," he said. He had been preparing the way for anti-locust patrols among the tribesmen of Somaliland. "We weren't paying them enough or something. They didn't give a damn about the locusts, anyway—they were food for them, not pests. They broke into my tent. Queensberry rules." Kicheko put up his fists. "No good. Spear straight through my arm. Dropped my Queensberry guard and got another spear in the lung. I knew it was my lung because frothy stuff came out. My blokes got me away in the jeep and I spent nine months in hospital at Mogadishu. White nuns there. Fed me rum and honey, ha ha ha!"

Ba Allen seemed to have avoided the sordid-liaison-with-a-native-girl syndrome. His liaisons had been farflung, free, and fertile.

"Got an eighteen-year-old daughter in Addis," he remarked. "Very pretty girl. Blood of Haile Selassie in her. Wants to come and look after me." He lived on Lamu, an island just off the Kenyan coast. "Got a son set up in donkey transport on Manda—next island from Lamu. Does jolly well. Looks after his donkeys. One wife in Northumbria and one, er, in Nairobi, I think. How many of my children in Lamu? Difficult to know, so many die. Four. Yes, four. Two of my brothers there too. They don't like England, never go back. I love it. Doesn't change, you know. You can still get lost in the bluebells!" A mess of rice was passed into the dinghy. "Ah," said Ba Allen, "jolly good bun shop this." His views on life were disarmingly tolerant. He did not waste his breath moralising.

"A lot of young people come to Lamu for the marijuana," he said. "Funny stuff—makes me see battle pictures, not love stories like it's supposed to. Take some of it and I'd walk into the back of a bus, probably get run over. My son went to school here. Read Modern Languages at Oxford but his heart was in painting. He was a lecturer at Stanford but he wanted to paint so he did, on the pavement at Palo Alto or something.

127

A chap saw him there and admired his work. He said, 'I'll fill this boy with marijuana and make an artist of him,' and he did. Make £50,000 a picture now. That's where I was introduced to it.

"Drinking? Yes, done some pretty intensive drinking out here. Generally after a fight.

"Some young men stay in Lamu and become Islamised. Most of the girls here insist on it. Damn pretty too. Most of them move on though. Young enthusiasm. Children—yes, good to have children. I told my son, he's got a young girl, about nineteen, she ran away from a Mexican convent, have a child. It's not necessary to be married as long as you let the mother see it occasionally, ha! ha! ha!" I wondered why the old man didn't fly from Mombasa to Lamu instead of roughing it on the dhow.

"I like this jahazi life," he said. "It's nice and peaceful. Not like sailing in England where you get knotted ropes flung at you. Actually I've just been to book a ticket on an aeroplane; I'm going back to England in the spring. Love it. Wouldn't mind staying there now. Just move from widow to widow—you can't stay with widows for too long, ha! ha! ha! Charming ladies.

"Want to be in Piccadilly on May Day—look for a maypole. Then I'll go to Henley. There's a gypsy feast in Cumbria in the middle of June. Come back to Lamu in September." I helped him to stand. "I'll have a shit while she's calm, I think." He was still laughing as he clambered into the wooden framework hung off the stern. His voice ignored the darkness.

"When I die," he said, "I don't want this bloody heaven business. I just want a small cloud near the earth so that I can smell the flowers and hear the nonsense talked in pubs. And I'll be sent on missions to places that I've known and loved." He was an amazing man. On the reverse side of his visiting card there was a statement made by Chief Joseph of the Nez Perce Indians of the north-western United States. The words are often quoted, but if they are wise or not I do not know.

128

"As I walk through this land," Chief Joseph had said, "I ask that the gods show me the ways of quiet so after my passing no one or no thing will have known of my being there."

I must say that I am glad that Ba Allen had ignored the ways of quiet when we were together on that dhow.

13

My one hundred per cent favourite African bird is the bateleur eagle. We were not in bateleur country yet, although with the mountains now just in sight above the southern horizon we soon would be, but we did see several specimens of another bird that I like because it has such a beautiful name. It is called the chanting goshawk. These birds tend to sit alone along the road-sides of West Africa, flashing their lobster socks at passers-by and frowning down their beaks. Their limbs come in a virulent and unnatural range of colour, shading from lifeboat orange to a Bette Davis red, and they can be quite startling at first sight. Waz happened to be pouring out our noon brew on the fifth day south of Gambaru when another leggy bird, this time in light-grey morning dress, strutted into view. It had red eyes.

"What's that?" said Waz. I looked up from my wrinkled copy of *Teach Yourself Hausa*, something that I was thoroughly failing to do.

"What's what?"

"That bird," said Waz, but it had gone. He described it.

"Probably a bustard," I said. We had already seen several in the area. Later in the afternoon Waz saw the same sort of bird again.

"Oh," I said, "it's a secretary bird."

Secretary birds eat snakes which they trample to death with their feet, and they have a pair of feathers reminiscent of quill pens sticking out roughly where their ears would be if they had any, hence their odd name. Waz produced a lengthy joke involving serpents in a typing pool—he actually wondered if luncheon vouchers would cover a cobra sandwich; we both seemed to be retreating somewhat into fantasy and memory, I probably more so than he. Walking for six or ten hours a day across a relatively uniform surface did leave a lot of one's brain untaxed, a situation to which the contents of my own skull had adapted quickly. My head was quite happy to neutralise itself with the cerebral equivalent of a tabloid and a Thermos flask, nostalgically flicking through its stock of old film. The most popular re-run was called "Women I Have Known". There was always a delicious surprise in realising that someone had been forgotten and she would be retrieved instantly from the memory banks, to be turned over and savoured in every recoverable detail.

Waz, by contrast, tended to think of the future. He was in the process of planning a house for his mother, an old lady almost blind with glaucoma. Waz had reached the age where bachelor quarters in someone else's compound were in-appropriate, and, although he was not yet married, he wanted his own set-up, with his mother secure within it. He would have no great problem in raising the necessary funds from his kinsmen, and, since he was closely related to the present district headman of Gulak, he already had a house site reserved for him. He mumbled on about his plans for nearly the whole afternoon, addressing himself largely to Norman who showed very little interest.

"Think in the end I'll have a corrugated iron roof," he said, "but I'll try painting it white. As long as it doesn't peel off it should reflect most of the sun."

Waz had a real enthusiasm for the practicalities of con-struction. Traditional thatching, he said, is cool and cheap, but it is highly inflammable and not as durable as tin, which is perhaps less pleasing to the eye. Tin also transmits heat with depressing efficiency, a fact discovered by young subalterns arriving from England at the beginning of the century, to join the newly formed West African Frontier Force. They came by sea to hulks anchored in the Niger delta and steamed up-river as berths in smaller boats were available. The minutiae of daily life in the force were recorded by F. P. Crozier in his book *Five Years Hard*, from which the following passage is an extract.

"'I don't think much of this place,' says Binger talking of Lokoja.

'What's the matter with it?' asks Miller.

'Look at that house, what is it?' asks Binger with a contemptuous smile. 'Why tin in the tropics?'

'That's the Niger Company stores,' says Miller. 'Tin doesn't wear out.'

'But what about the poor devils who work in the heat under the tin, don't they wear out?' asks Binger."

The Boer War was not yet over but volunteers from many units were applying to join the Frontier Force. The main attractions were polo and the possibility of dousing Fulani cavalry with lead. Lieutenant Berty Porter of the 19th Hussars was among the first arrivals, and he had the regulations formally read to him by the Officer-in-Charge of the hulk on which he was waiting.

"'On behalf of the medical department,' announced the officer, 'I wish to say that you are advised to take five grains of quinine a day as a preventative against malaria, drink only boiled and filtered water, and refrain from intercourse with native women.'"

Waz and I took a couple of Nivaquine pills each week as our preventative against malaria, but drinking only boiled water was impossible. We needed gallons of the stuff every day and could not afford to spend hours over our cooking pots, nor could we hang about waiting for the sterilised but scalding water to cool down. Young Berty Porter solved the problem by, apparently, dispensing with the need for drinking water altogether.. His planned liquid intake for a six month stint in the bush was as follows:

"'Let me see,' says Porter. 'Six months. Roughly a hundred and eighty days—a hundred and eighty bottles of whisky, fifteen dozen, that sounds awful—half that amount of gin—a bottle of Angostura, a case of beer—four dozen—a case of champagne, and that should do.' " Strangely enough Lt. Porter survived and was promoted to the rank of captain for his efforts at the storming of Bida in December 1900.

As for the medical officer's third piece of advice to Berty Porter, I, for one, had not shared a sleeping mat with anyone at all for quite some time and I assessed my immediate chances of so doing as roughly nil. I was not an attractive sight. It is true that I was deeply tanned, but next to Waz I looked like a snowball and a syphilitic one at that. Every few days the skin would peel off my nose in big, white flakes like false but suggestive receipts for the wages of sin. I was also very grimy in between baths at waterholes, and my wardrobe was way out of fashion. In this regard my shorts deserve description. They were very old and navy blue and there was a great deal of them. They rose from knee to navel in sexless propriety, exceeding my waist measurement by at least six inches, and, with the help of a penknife, some string, and *Scouting for Boys* would have converted to a snug tent. The threadbare label read as follows:

Size No. 4

WAIST 36 in.

HEY & FLOOKTON

1943

The Flooktons had seen my father through the last years of the war, and they would see me through Nigeria, with neither flies nor pockets to distract me from my manly quest. Inside them I was safe, ignored if not quite shunned by women of whatever kind. Indeed, I met a very nice one some days later, but my trusty Flooktons kept me pure. The lady's name was Gloria and she had a cutting wit.

"Wow!" she said as I had appeared, knees primly covered and ragged plimsolls flapping. "Shorts by back and sides, shoes by Empire Maid!"

The damper sections of the plain were now sprouting narrow strips of forest, with even some lianas hanging from the trees. Most of the natural vegetation had long been cleared for farms but we had, in theory anyway, left the Sudan savannah behind and were well into the next vegetation zone, which is called northern Guinea savannah. The grasses were taller and the trees less thorny. The rainfall would be roughly that of south-east England, about thirty inches a year, but all falling in a wet season of three to four months. Maize and millet had been replaced by sorghum as the main crop, and it was now more or less all harvested. Since the main danger to ripe grain on the savannahs is from pests rather than from fickle weather, there is no great urgency about bringing in the crop, and the actual harvest can extend over a month or more. Unlike the general stampede at sowing time there is no sudden rush to cut the grain but a gradual in-gathering of a few baskets here and a bundle there. The corn stalks themselves are up to eight feet long and are used to make fences and for rough thatching jobs, as well as fodder.

The vine Leocarpus with its slender, lanceolate leaves had become less common, but a heavy, segmented growth called *Cissus quadragularis* now dangled from many of the trees, obscuring its hosts in strings of sausage shaped cactus. A whole tree festooned with cissus looked like a knotty old gladiator who had at last met his match in a tank of Superglue and octopus.

Our olfactory organs were again stimulated after the bare and almost unperfumed grasslands. Some of the vegetation was sweetly scented, but some of it stank. There was one especially bad pong which took us ages to locate. It came from the tiny green flowers of a spiny bush whose name I have not discovered. We became quite adept at picking it out and would hold our breaths until well past it. We were once more among a Kanuri population, engaged, as it happened, in weeding the late guinea corn. The main crop is harvested in October and November but a dwarf variety can be planted at the end of the rains in those places where enough soil water is retained. The southern plains were already green with yard high fronds between which the backs of the peasantry were bent to the everlasting job of hoeing.

Apart from the inevitable voting booths, each village had at least one small tin hut belching smoke from the front and flour from the back. Diesel driven mills are quickly replacing female muscle power as the means of reducing grain to flour, and instead of gathering round a wooden mortar, village women can now hang about the mill sheds while their daily ration is ground. There was usually a wonderful collection of decorated calabashes piled beside the shed doorways, each containing the day's grain for one family. Every so often a hand would mysteriously draw a calabash in at one entrance and push out a bowl of flour at the other. One occasionally caught a complete glimpse of the millers when they could take the fumes and the heat no more. They would emerge like dazed ghosts, white with dust, or, when their charges had broken down, smeared with a paste of grease and soot. I wondered if the diesel-men had yet acquired the dubious reputation of the traditional European miller. How long would it be until their customers, so recently freed from the daily chore of pounding grain, by-passed the village mills altogether and bought their flour in shops? A few more generations, perhaps, or just a few more years?

Wrecked primary schools were another common architectural feature of the southern plains villages, the silent ruins of, perhaps, a bygone age and culture. In fact the schools were the silent ruins of an age and culture yet to come. The word was that the building contractors had ripped off everyone in sight, the structures being sub-standard right the way from the breeze blocks to the paint. Twisted roofs and broken walls lay where the wet season storms had left them and some shattered classrooms still had writing on the blackboards. The physical destruction of the schools was not actually such a terrible blow since, in the long dry season, classes were held in the shade of the nearest large tree. In any case the Kanuri are a conservative lot, not entirely convinced that Education is a Good Thing, and nor, I suspected, were many of the teachers so convinced. The ones that we saw in the area were mostly boys in their early twenties who would come zooming after us on their bicycles, their watches and their sunglasses flashing. They seemed to spend their days polishing up their shiny bits and dreaming of a transfer.

Occasionally we passed settlements that seemed foreign. There was something about the way that the huts were clustered, a slight change in the style of thatching, perhaps, that gave the impression of a different order. The inhabitants of these places actually looked a little different, too. They were generally quite short and somewhat ragged, the women in grimy cotton skirts and the men often in nothing more than loincloths. They or their parents had come down from the hills now showing blue above the horizon, and we had a rough assessment of them from a man whom we met on the sixth day after leaving Gambaru. He was about sixty and his name was Kurso. He lived in the village of Burni which was a mixture of Kanuri compounds and Shuwa byres. We chose the Shuwa section. Kurso's hut happened to be the first one that we came to and luckily he spoke good Fulani.

"He's from Mora," said Waz, "over in the Cameroons. They all speak Fulani there. He thinks you're a Syrian."

"Syrian?"

"Yeah, you've got pretty brown."

While we unloaded and hobbled the donkeys a woman brought a bowl of tuwo and sauce for Kurso. He did not invite us to share it, which was odd, and he seemed to be eating rather awkwardly. I then noticed that he had no fingers. He was a leper.

I filled our mugs with tea and thinking that Kurso might like some too I offered him what was left in the pot. The niceties of afternoon tea parties were rather distant from my thoughts when Waz stopped me.

"Give him a mug," he said. "It's an insult giving him the pot. Cooking things are for women, you know. Grown men don't lick out their wives' pots." I felt exceedingly stupid and groped around for something to say. The surrounding byres had filled.

"Nice cows," I said, "are they all his?"

"No," said Waz. "He says that none of them are. He had to sell all his because of his hands. He couldn't herd cows himself and he's got no sons to do it for him. He can't afford to pay anyone either. He says a herdboy costs ten pounds a month." Some boys, I knew, would herd cattle for nothing, but would be given a calf after nine months' or a year's service.

"He's asking if you're a Muslim," Waz said. "I told him that you're a European." Kurso continued to speak. "He says that he's a Shuwa Arab and so you and he are cousins." Waz thought for a moment. "Funny," he said, "my mother says exactly the same thing about Arabs and Europeans.

"Gar! He's just saying what my mother always used to tell us about why Europeans have so many things. It's what nearly all the ordinary people think. He says that once all we humans used to be the same until God decided to offer us the choice between having the Kingdom of Heaven when we die, or having the riches of the earth now. We Africans and the Muslims chose to wait and go to heaven, but the Europeans refused that choice and took this world now, which is why they make all these wonderful things. But they refused heaven. He says that although you are a European yourself and you won't go to Paradise, at least you're not a blacksmith."

No matter what the tribe, almost all West African societies hold their blacksmiths as a caste apart, often, but not always, of lower status than the peasantry. I find this odd because, until the relatively recent introduction of metal from outside, the blacksmith not only hammered tools and weapons, but actually produced the iron as well. Without iron, two of man's principal activities, viz. agriculture and warfare, would have been severely curtailed, yet the men who made these things possible, and even their non-practising descendants, are widely despised. I asked Kurso if he would allow a female relative to marry one.

"Never," he said. "Better to marry a pagan from the hills than a smith."

"Why?" I asked.

"Smiths are bad people," said Kurso. "They work at the forge and they get the black stuff from the fire into their hearts. You can't go to heaven with a black heart." Kurso also had some good theories about the Borroro Fulanis. They were not entirely "people of the book", by which he meant good Muslims, because they did not give alms, but they were nevertheless children of God.

"We Shuwa call them Red Ants, because they grow wings and they fly away in the rains like termites. They came into the world after Adam and Eve started to grow gourds. God saw the gourds growing and he turned the beautiful ones into Fulanis. The ugly ones became the pagans in the hills and you people who do not pray."

Kurso had a small charcoal brazier on which he sprinkled a few sticks of a grass called goye in the Shuwa language. It smoked with a sweet smell. We talked on over more tea and light refreshment of kola nuts and bulls' eyes.

"If blacksmiths are bad people, what about Europeans?" I asked. "I mean Europeans make all sorts of things in metal—cars, aeroplanes, everything."

"Oh," said Kurso, "cars and planes are knowledge handed down from the prophet David. In any case, Europeans don't work bellows, so they don't get dirty inside. Anyhow I myself have only been a maigardi or a gardener in my life, and so I don't know the work of Europeans."

We crossed the first contour for about three maps soon after leaving Kurso's compound. The thin brown line ran north-west to south-east, illustrating a subdued and unremarkable feature called the Bama Ridge. This fifty-thousand-year-old tide mark is probably the highest of Lake Chad's former shore lines, but a cyclist who passed us had hardly to lift his backside off the saddle as he reached the sandy crest. Beyond that lay another afternoon of imperceptibly rising plain until dramatic squiggles representing Mandara burst right across the map. The "A" sides of the dozen sheets that we had already crossed were not exactly cluttered, and had been in places indistinguishable from their plain white backing. I had, on short occasions, even followed creases in the paper, taking them for tracks. At all events, I am a lousy map reader, but here at last was a proper message from the cartographer, and one to be taken seriously since mistakes among the hills would be a dreadful slog to correct. I was, however, greatly relieved to have something appetising to look at after the blank doldrums of Bornu, now so nearly over.

We stopped for lunch at a place called Zongo, and had a celebratory wash in the village waterhole. A couple of marabou storks watched morosely as Waz and I sloshed about with bowlfuls of the opaque water. We dined on our inevitable rice and pilchards, sharing our meal with a Shuwa in whose compound we had dumped the gear. The Shuwa was about sixty and had made the fatal mistake of divorcing his only wife. He had not managed to replace her and had retired to contemplate the future from the iron bedstead on which we found him. He was actually reclining beneath a pink mosquito net, but he dug out a spoon from the tin trunk under his bed and he joined us to eat on the floor.

Our route was slowly converging with the main Maiduguri to Yola highway, and we actually hit the tarmac at Pulke, a village lying under the very tip of the hills. We might have been approaching Cornwall from the Atlantic. Boulder strewn slopes leapt straight from the plain to an ascending chain of hills lying head-on to us and running south in a widening peninsula. The map described a gnarled and crooked finger rising from knuckle to knuckle in a broken series of jagged peaks, culminating in the smooth fist of the Cameroonian Plateau some twenty miles away. The main road swung west round the highlands to service the towns of Gwoza, Madagali, Gulak, Michika, and Mubi, bowling across the littoral where hill emerged from plain. The settlements themselves were like so many resorts dotted along a sea shore, to which the hill men of the interior were increasingly attracted.

For the first ten or fifteen miles south of Pulke we would be travelling down the eastern edge of the hills with an ever broadening wedge of mountain between us and the main Yola road on the western side. When we reached a suitable break we would climb up to the spine from which we would be able to look down into Nigeria to the west and the Cameroons in the east. We would, as far as possible, follow the crest south on to and over the Cameroonian Plateau whose broken edge falls away in jumbled confusion to the Nigerian Plain.

The names of over two dozen different clans were printed over the first twelve miles of charted hill. The small area of the Mandaras harbours more than thirty different ethnic units, most of which do not exceed ten thousand members. A few, like the Kapsiki of the Cameroonian Plateau, count more than a hundred thousand. This was hill-billy country with a vengeance, a land of deep and twisting glens curling among steep and paradoxically well populated bens. The first major break in the highlands would be at Mubi, about eighty miles south of Pulke. There the River Yedseram descends from the plateau and begins its long and dusty progress north across the Chad Basin which, with our arrival in Pulke that evening, we had at long last crossed.

We reached the outlying compounds at sunset and met a little girl bouncing along the track with a pot of water on her head. She saw me, screamed, and fled, the resulting cascade a transient splash of gold in the evening light. I suppose that she had taken me for the local bogey man. Waz picked up the jar and a chap pointed out the girl's compound from his perch up a nearby tree. He was up there securing his hay for the dry season, a customary storage practice whereby long plaits of

140

grass are wedged across the stoutest boughs. Norman snatched absently at a trailing strand and brought down the lot, but luckily without the chap. We helped to put the hay back and proceeded with the jar. Our plan was to leave the donkeys in care locally and to rest for some days ourselves, Waz in Gulak and I in Maiduguri. It happened to be a Friday and I needed to do what I call "Monday Things", involving, in this case, banks and my passport, which, I hoped, would by now contain an extension to my visa.

Waving the little girl's pot we entered the unfenced compound. The bare ground was awash with sorghum heads, a pile of which was under attack by six young men armed with what at first I thought were crutches. In fact their flails looked more like crude ice hockey sticks. The lads themselves were in the usual assortment of clothes, ranging from "I-don't-know-how-they-wear-them-in-this-heat" nylon shirts and spray-on bell bottoms to traditional smocks and homespun cotton shorts. A simple platform, supported five feet off the ground on twisted poles, stood behind the threshing area. It was stacked high with peanut vines which from a distance looked like bundled hops. Underneath it were a couple of tyres in the twilight of their final incarnation. One of them contained a nasty little dog and the other housed two infants. There is a road into the Cameroons at Pulke and the village thus accumulates such jetsam of the highway.

The visa and the bank note side of travelling in Africa is a big bad scene as many would agree, but there are delightful compensations. That evening, for example, we had a clear demonstration of how quickly one's problems can be solved if they are of the country. Within five minutes of handing back the water pot our gear had been stowed inside an empty hut and water had been provided for our refreshment, while our transport division was already breaking wind in an ecstasy of hay and old corn stalks.

The little girl's father was called Usman Dare, and although his aged parents were still alive he was the de facto compound head. He was happy to look after the donkeys for a few days, and had actually taken us for refugees, running from the war in Chad. He was most sympathetic.

"I know the fire behind you," he said as he tethered the mokes. Fortunately he was speaking in metaphor, because the slightest spark within range of the flatulent Claude would have blown us all sky high.

14

I spent the weekend with my friends in Maiduguri and on Monday I discovered that my passport was still "being processed". This meant either an indefinite wait, or another trip from somewhere en route to collect it. The next natural break would be fairly close to Mubi, about halfway down the mountain chain, and I decided not to wait but to return to Maiduguri again from there. In the meantime we would be making only short incursions into the Cameroons and I just hoped that no one would catch us. The border was, after all, unmarked and more or less unpatrolled.

While I was in Maiduguri I attended a lecture on birds at the university. I learnt that of the approximately 8,000 species throughout the world some 664 are indigenous to Nigeria. Looking around the lecture hall I noticed that of the approximately forty people present some half dozen were indigenes. The rest were what the *Observer's Book of Birds* would describe as "Migrants and Summer Visitors", and were a fairly representative sample of the journeymen academics found throughout the Third World.

The lecturer was showing some marvellous transparencies but I inevitably dozed off, actually losing consciousness at the sight of a spur-winged plover. Unfortunately I missed the birds of prey, coming-to midway through the hammerkop which, I learnt, eats nothing but the tadpoles of a frog called zenopus. I wondered how the hammerkop could tell one sort of tadpole from another, but fell asleep again before I could think of an answer.

All this repose set me fair for a good piss-up and instead of going straight back to meet Waz in Gulak I stopped off in Gwoza for the night. I had immoderate plans involving a pair of teachers there, a fridge and lots of alcohol. The teachers' names were Gloria and Laurel. Gloria has already been mentioned in connection with my shorts and she shared a bungalow with Laurel in the compound of Gwoza Secondary School. Three other guests were being entertained by the girls as I arrived and their names were Sylvester, Dave and Frank.

Dave was short, Welsh, and incomprehensible. He ran a nearby quarry. He left within five minutes of my arriving, closely followed by Frank, who had had a bad weekend. Being fresh from Canada and only just out of school, Frank's mind was still skiddooing round clean lavabos and looking for the chain; it had not yet made the dissociations necessary for its continuing tranquillity. Each slice of bread, for example, was still a disappointment, since Frank had not scraped off the assumption of what one might call an on-going butter situation. He still assumed that basins included taps and plugs, and, naively, water. Poor boy. He was physically an apparent blend of stuff that grows in caves and under flower pots, except that his bottom lip was throbbing and bright scarlet. Sylvester had smacked him in the mouth.

Sylvester was also fresh from Canada, but in this case not a native, having come originally from Czechoslovakia in 1968. He sat for another hour, blinking through his glasses and wiping off the sweat. He seemed hardly the type to hand out knuckle sandwiches and I assumed that Nigeria had unsettled him. He finally left, having just popped over from his own bungalow to deliver Gloria's birthday card. He had made a slight mistake and had addressed it to "Groria". She opened the envelope and said, "Oh no!"

I knew what Sylvester had written. He was that sort of guy—late forties, unmarried, lonely as hell and a pain in the neck. He had only been in Gwoza for a week, having flown out to take up a teaching job. I suppose it was like a clearing in the jungle to him and there was Groria in the middle waiting to be rescued. Unfortunately Sylvester wasn't what you would call a swinger and his liana-work let him down with a crash. She said, "No."

Neither Waz nor I was in a particular hurry to resume play and so when I met him in Gulak the following morning we decided that time-out would continue for another day. I had noticed that donkeyloads of pots would sometimes clip down through the village to the road, accumulating beneath the mango trees until a willing lorry came along to carry them to market. I was intrigued and so we borrowed a couple of wobbly bicycles and set off on the trail, ending up with sore bums at a place called Wakara some fifteen miles back into the foothills. Waz had an uncle living there whose name was Wafundumta and whose two remaining teeth hung from his gums like long lost golf tees. He had curly white hairs in his eyebrows, but despite his age (he was about fifty), his facial expressions were those of a mischievous little boy. We dumped the bikes in his compound and he led us on another couple of miles, pointing out deserted hut sites and the abandoned fields once cultivated by members of Waz's extended family. Almost the entire population had decamped to resettle in places like Gulak, but Wafundumta had stayed behind. I gather that he had rather let the side down by marrying a blacksmith's daughter.

Waz's was an aristocratic family. His grandfather had been the district headman of Gulak in colonial times and, before the establishment of *pax Britannica*, had been a respected fighting man. He was now well over ninety and had fathered somewhere in the region of one hundred and fifty children. My visit to him in Gulak had been more like an audience than a casual "hallo", but his nephew Wafundumta lacked the family's blue-blooded look. Although he was unusually tall his eyes were far too twinkly to belong to a pillar of society.

The name Wafundumta is actually a question in the Marghi language and it means "Who is angry?" Children in many African societies are given names according to a circumstance of birth, not in the Running-Bear or He-Who-Catches-Many-Buffalo style, but as a kind of talisman against misfortune or "bad thoughts". "Who is angry?" could perhaps be better translated as "Who minds?" or "Who is jealous?", implying that a member of the community, living or dead, may have had cause to resent Wafundumta's birth. Such names are not so much a description of the child itself as a comment upon its social environment. Usman Dare, the man who was looking after our donkeys in Pulke, was called Zuara in his people's own language. Zuara means "Just he alone". The mortality rate for children under five is extremely high in the Mandaras, exceeding fifty per cent in some areas, and the name "Just he alone" is an apology to the ancestors for there being no other children to honour them, despite many births. Childbirth is so dangerous a time for mother and infant that expectant mothers are often referred to by the Marghi as "dead women". It has been suggested that this practice predicts, as it were, an unhappy eventuality, and thus provides some measure of control over the situation.

We arrived at an isolated group of huts perched on and between some massive boulders at the head of a small valley. The compound was stiff with pots and people. Men of all ages were lolling about on the rocks and women of all ages were hard at it under woven grass shelters, banging out the ceramics. In fairness, the men had their industry too, since this was a family of practising smiths, but apart from guzzling copious draughts of beer they were not particularly occupied that day.

The compound patriarch was called Waida, which means "Who trusts me?", and while he touched up the spear heads which Waz and I had brought for repair, I watched the potters. The women chipped clay up by the basketful from great pits which had been mined for many years, following veins of clay along the dry stream beds and between the lower rocks. The clay was softened and kneaded to the right consistency and then bonked into shape by the "log-and-stonker" method. A suitable dollop of clay would be hit with a fist sized stone against a slightly concave surface, either an old grinding stone or the hollowed end of an upturned log, the lump being turned all the while and gradually taking on a spherical shape. The trick was to keep the clay to a uniform thickness, as it tended to splurge out if it was hit too hard. When the pots had been sun dried and were firm enough the necks were added and a glaze was brushed on. They were then burnished with a string of baobab seeds to achieve a good colour and fired in a quick blaze of dry grass.

Wafundumta talked all the way back to the bicycles. He was telling us more about the exploits of Waz's grandfather who appeared to have been a pretty lethal individual. Although the Mandaras are home to dozens of different language groups, the hill people all have a broadly similar attitude to violence. The rules of contact were more or less uniform and, according to the best authorities, were hardly ever broken. Close relatives were clubbed with only wooden objects, weapons of metal being reserved for more distant kinsmen. All restraint was lifted for unrelated men of other villages who were met with missiles coated in various poisons.

We re-entered Wafundumta's compound and he disappeared into a hut. He emerged several minutes later and bounded into the open with a ghastly shriek, looking like a cross between a survivor of Rorke's Drift and the Battle of Hastings. He was eighty per cent hidden by a huge oxhide shield but the whites of his eyes kept bobbing round the edges in a grown-up game of peekaboo. His red felt hat stuck straight up in the air and a bunch of small antelope horns was rattling at his waist. These contained charms and potions whose function was to protect the wearer against the more unfortunate results of combat. Round his body Wafundumta had wound a long white cheese-cloth but I do not know why. Besides his long and slender spear he had an appalling kind of sickle with a spike, very roughly in the shape of a letter F, to be used for close-up chopping at the enemy. He went through the entire Marghi drill book, prancing across the open ground with his wife in immediate and vociferous support. She got thoroughly excited, ululating and dancing right behind him with a bit of impromptu tambourine work on a rusted-out circle of an old enamel bowl. It was definitely a team performance and although the enamel bowl and Wafundumta's plastic shoes let the twentieth century right in, it was authentic. Warfare in the hills actually used to be like that.

Engagements were ideally a set piece, with the two sides (often two halves of the same village) meeting on a traditionally accepted site, their women lined up behind them to cheer, jeer or wail, and the old men looking on with advice for the combatants. Sallies might continue throughout the day until darkness or a fatality broke up the party. There were no overall strategies, no commanders, nor any manoeuvring of coherent bodies. A man would simply pick an enemy and attempt to nail him with spear, bow or whatever was to hand. The whole performance was held more in the spirit of an amateur rugby football match than as warfare is conducted today. The aim was never to conquer territory, but to enjoy the exhilaration of contact sport and to show off. The excuse was usually a tiff over women but was entirely unimportant to the majority of fighters.

The last recorded conflict in the Wakara area took place just over the Cameroonian border in the Kapsiki village of Mogode. There have been minor clashes since but, before Independence, the British administrators managed to pacify their part of the Mandaras by confiscating all the shields they could find. They did not get every one, of course. A consequence of the traditional state of mutual hostility was that each clan became isolated from the next, and men were more or less restricted to a small area of hill where they lived out what, to the lowlanders, appeared to be violent and mysterious lives. In keeping with the hill tradition of individual responsibility each man behaved largely as a law unto himself, with none of the almost feudal restraints of the Muslim plains. Today the whole area is administered by local authorities and village and district headmen run the show, but in the past the only widespread institution of authority was vested in the persons of certain priest-kings whose power transcended village and language groups and influenced people over a wide area. The scholar Antony Kirk-Greene has recorded examples of how the Llidi or priest-king of Sukur used his power. Sukur is in the hills behind Madagali.

> In 1930, at the beginning of the scourge of locusts, the Llidi collected one penny from every male in the Mandara region and from many villages beyond, British and French. The purpose of this fund was to enable the Sukur smiths to smelt enough iron so that their colleagues at Guduf might construct a cauldron which would confine all the locusts in the world. The people of Sukur itself made a special contribution of one gown, one sheep and one cone of salt each . . . the plague, however, continued on its usual seven year cycle and voices were not lacking to explain the failure of the Llidi's supernatural powers by the "regrettable" British prohibition of the final rite of sacrificing two virgins.

The Muslims of Bornu traditionally regarded the hill people as a bunch of savages. They gave them names like Kirdi, which means "faithless ones" and Matakam, meaning "God will ensure that I avoid them". Islamic and Christian influences now dominate Kirdi society but it is the pagan roots of Kirdi life which still intrigue the European visitor to the area. The Germans, who first "administered" the hills south of Gwoza, installed one Hamman Yaji as the district headman in 1902. He established himself in a mud walled fort at Madagali and for the next twenty-five years he pursued a successful career as regional terrorist and slave dealer. His German masters were replaced by the British who assumed responsibility for the area, known as northern Adamawa, under a League of Nations Mandate in 1923. It took the Brits four years to discover the grisly secrets of Hamman Yaji's rule, recorded for posterity in the tyrant's diary. The entry for 16 August 1917 describes a fairly typical day in the life of a despot.

"I sent Fad-el-Allah with his men to raid Sukur [about fifteen miles away]. They captured eighty slaves, of whom I gave away forty. We killed twenty-seven men and women and seventeen children."

The Sukur people had some fairly nasty habits themselves. The Llidi required a certain number of eunuchs to fill established posts, the Guardian of the Royal Children was an example, and his llagama, or head smith, was the principal castrator. Many of Hamman Yaji's male prisoners were sent up to Sukur for gelding, to return as custodians of the harem. Two victims of this treatment were still alive when Antony Kirk-Greene toured the district in the mid-1950s.

Behind the Llidi's house is a small rock on which the operation was always performed. An eye witness described how the wretched man was placed sitting on the edge of the stone, his hands bound to a stake in front of him and his legs forced wide apart by four slaves, with another four grasping his body. At the Sukur surgery (if the word is not too magnanimous) the practice was to cut out the testicles with a small iron blade then pour hot oil on the wound. If it healed at all the eunuch would be on duty within two weeks. The present Llagama was acknowledged as an expert but the casualty rate was enormous. [He] told me that [he] expected to lose ninety per cent of his cases.

Travel in the hills was restricted under the provisions of the Unsettled Districts Ordinance until well after the Second World War, but even before that there had been very little peaceful contact between the plains and the hills. Middle-men did pass between the two, trading in cloth, salt and iron, but the earliest European explorers found themselves accompanying slave raids, or ghrazzies as they were called, if they wished to go into the mountains. Dixon Denham rode south with a ghrazzie (and a slightly troubled conscience) in April 1823. He assumed that the hills he was about to penetrate were the fabled Mountains of the Moon, but he was unable to confirm this because the raid went disastrously wrong. Denham's account is in the characteristically stiff-upper-lip style of Victorian narrative, but he gives a hair raising account of the final battle of the campaign. The Kanuri army had moved south, out of

Bornu, collecting tribute from minor sultanates and emirdoms on the way. There had been several routine attacks on defence-less villages, whose inhabitants had been raped and pillaged in the normal way, before the main body reached a large and well defended Mandara settlement. The Arabs who had escorted Denham all the way from Tripoli were beside themselves with desire for booty and,

> without any support from the Bornu troops and notwith-standing the showers of arrows, some poisoned, carried the palisades, driving the [Kirdis] up the sides of the hills. The women were everywhere seen supplying their protectors with fresh arrows and when they retreated to the hills, still shooting, they assisted by rolling down huge masses of rock previously undermined which killed several of the Arabs.

The fighting was not entirely chivalrous—"about one hundred of the Bornu spearmen pierced through and through some fifty unfortunates who were left wounded near the palisades". The Bornuese also took casualties: "Three times I saw the man transfixed to earth who was dismounted for the purpose of firing the town . . ." The Kirdis counter-attacked. Denham's horse was badly wounded.

> . . . an arrow struck me in the face as it passed . . . I had two sticking in my bornouse. The Arabs had suffered terribly . . . one dropped near me with five arrows sticking in his head alone . . . we instantly became a flying mass . . . I was following at a round gallop in the steps of one of the Eunuchs, his face expressive of great dismay, when my horse stumbled and fell . . . the Kirdis were upon me; I had, however, kept hold of the bridle and seizing a pistol from the holsters, I presented it at two of these ferocious savages who were pressing me with their spears . . . [but] . . . another received the contents [of the pistol] . . . somewhere in his left shoulder . . . I again pushed my retreat.

Denham's horse came down again, and it escaped before he could remount, leaving him on foot and unarmed. The eunuch and four others were butchered and stripped before his eyes. "Their cries were dreadful . . . my pursuers made several thrusts that badly wounded my hands and slightly my body . . . they were alone prevented from murdering me by the fear of not injuring the value of my clothes." They seem to have forgotten that value in the heat of the moment, though, because Denham's shirt was torn off his back. "I was left perfectly naked . . . when my plunderers began to quarrel I crept under the belly of the horse nearest me and started as fast as my legs would carry me . . . the prickly underwood tore at my flesh." Denham escaped across a stream but not before, horror of horrors, "under my hand a large liffa, the worst kind of serpent this country produces, rose from its coil . . . I tumbled headlong into the water beneath."

Dixon Denham, stark naked, assessed his position. "The forlorn and wretched situation in which I was . . . flashed with all its force upon my imagination. I had already begun to plan my night's rest in the top of one of the tamarind trees when the idea of liffas . . . excited a shudder of despair." At that moment he saw horsemen through the trees. They were Bornuese.

"Marmay . . . the sheik's negro . . . assisted me to mount behind him, while the arrows whistled over our heads and we then galloped off to the rear as fast as his wounded horse could carry us."

They reached a river.

"On coming to the stream the horses, with blood gushing from their nostrils, rushed into the shallow water. I knelt down amongst them and seemed to imbibe new life by the copious draughts of the muddy beverage which I swallowed . . . the effect produced on the horses that were wounded by poisoned arrows was extraordinary: immediately after drinking they dropped and instantly died." Eight days later the survivors of the raid straggled back to Bornu.

Denham was rather disappointed. "Of the Mandara chain,

and its surrounding incumbent hills, though full of interest, I regret my inability to give a more perfect account."

He did, however, note that the Kirdi girls captured from the hills on more successful forays were, for negresses, "the most pleasing and perfectly formed" that he had seen. The slaves he describes were all under sixteen, "yet quite women, for these are precocious climes". The Kirdi girls were selected "on the magnitude of those attractions for which their southern sisters are so celebrated . . . I have known a man about to make a purchase of one out of three, regardless of the charms of feature, turn their faces from him, and looking at them behind, just above their hips, as we dress a line of soldiers, make choice or her whose person most projected beyond that of her companions."

A large, white lorry was parked near Usman Dare's compound when we returned to Pulke after our five days' rest. The lorry was one of the mobile clinics which were for ever charging up and down the Yola road, exhorting the populace to come down for their injections. Outbreaks of all sorts of things were always sweeping the hills, but this year the cholera had been particularly bad. Why the hill people should be especially vulnerable I did not then know, but when I found a queue forming beside the lorry I joined it. No harm in a booster, I thought.

I felt slightly awkward as I waited in line. It wasn't just that I was white—I was used to being a physical freak by now—but I appeared to be miles taller than everyone else. It then struck me that the queue was entirely female, and, even for Africa, there were an awful lot of babies around. Being empty handed and at a temporary loss I retreated behind a cigarette and a fixed grin, ignoring the giggles and stares and much else about me.

"What fools the men are," I thought smugly. "Don't they realise that these shots are painless and for their own good?"

I reached the head of the queue and presented my arm. The vaccination gun hovered.

"Where your pickin?" said the male nurse.

"Pickin?" I said. I suddenly felt embarrassed. Everybody else had one except me. I re-offered my arm.

"Not good for you, Bature," said the male nurse. He was talking to me as if I were the village idiot. Of course it was good for me. I could contract cholera as soon as the next man, or woman come to that. The ladies stirred behind me and several little blobs began to squall.

"Look," I said to the guy, "just give me a shot, OK? I don't mind paying if that's the problem."

"This needle no good for you, Bature," said the nurse again. I groaned. Couldn't the man see that I was exactly the same as everyone else beneath the outer layers? I nearly told him that germs are colour blind.

"God damn it," I said. "You know there's a lot of cholera around. Why can't I have an injection like everyone else?"

The nurse gave me a withering stare. "This not cholera, Bature. This meningitis for small pickin."

I crawled away.

15

Our aim was to follow the spine of the Mandaras from start to finish and our first problem was to get into them. We skirted the eastern hills all morning and were passed by several Peugeots full of Cameroon bound Frenchmen in cowboy hats. We also met Mrs. Madame, Waz's aunt by marriage, who scrunched to a halt when she saw us. She had spent some years in the States where her husband had worked at the U.N., and she therefore qualified for the title "Madame", which had, by dint of common usage, become her accepted surname. She was on her way home having driven round the hills that morning from Gulak to inspect progress in the building of a new women teachers' college near the mission at Ngoshe, which is where we were going. Waving goodbye, she gunned her red Ford Escort back up the dirt road towards Pulke. From the hill tops she would have looked like a tiny red bead, rolling along a string the colour of faded jute.

Enormous holding tanks for the sorghum crop had been erected everywhere along the road. Propped up by short stakes these basin shaped granaries were made of grass matting and were open to the dry season skies. Their crisp newness was a delight to the eye and most of them were brimming over, the heads of grain rather attractively arranged and giving the whole structure the shape of an old hay rick. These grain stores were of a similar pattern to others made all over the savannahs, but in the few miles of dirt track which we had followed that morning I felt a subtle change in geography which I could not exactly pinpoint. It was something to do with the road. Although many of the villages we had been through on the journey were accessible to vehicles, few of them seemed to have absorbed the fact of a road, be it only a stretch of sand.

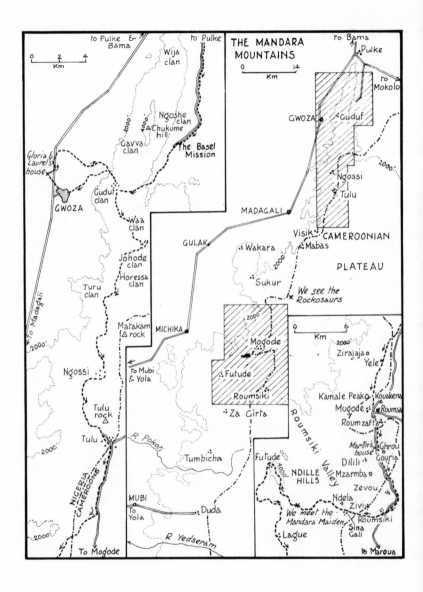

Footpaths would cross or run alongside but vehicle tracks seemed to remain strangers, lying outside the compound screens. Here below the mountains the road had suddenly become a village street, with people sitting on the stoops of rectangular mud huts giving directly to it. Shady trees were growing in a municipal sort of way and, although I should not exaggerate, this short and obscure stretch of road was like a breath of home. Perhaps the hill people, in their rather sudden liberation, had adapted more thoroughly to change than one might have at first supposed.

We passed a few schools set in scratchy playing fields and waved to children kicking real footballs, sure fire signs of Christian missionary influence. The first mission in the whole area was established at Gulak, over on the western side of the hills, in 1948, but the station at Ngoshe, which we were approaching, was not built until 1959. It had been an outpost of the Swiss based Basel mission to the Cameroons, but had joined forces with a Nigerian missionary society after the plebiscite of 1961 when the area had passed from U.N. trusteeship to become an official part of Nigeria. The buildings stood at the mouth of a small valley which ran back into the hills, giving access to an area of broken upland called Guduf. We planned to enter the hills by way of the valley, which was called Warawa Gavva, and to continue south, following the ridge of the Mandaras as closely as possible. We were accompanied for the last mile into Ngoshe by an urchin with a twisted foot who held my hand. As we passed a particularly big fig tree he mumbled something in Hausa.

"He says it's got spirits," said Waz.

"Yes," said the child, "it's got spirits. They killed my father last year. A branch fell on his head and then they covered him with water."

"Oh," we said, and walked on.

The mission house itself was a dark, two-storeyed structure of solid local stone and it reminded me of a north Pennine farmhouse, except for the smell. Nigerianisation had occurred some years before, but posters of Jesus and of Swiss chalets were still clinging faithfully to the walls. The ambient temperature was well into the nineties and a shoal of abandoned fish heads was jiving across the kitchen floor. They had obviously been leaping there for some considerable time and knew their way around. The filth was almost a physical shock to me, but the shower worked and I managed to avoid touching the walls. I stood under the water, thinking about cleanliness and godliness and laziness, and came to no definite conclusions, other than to remind myself, yet again, not to take things for granted or to assume that one thing necessarily led to another.

The Reverend was away in Mubi, but his wife was there and after our showers we whiled away the early afternoon with her. She was doing something domestic to a basketful of bean pods in the shade of a large mango tree, and was not overwhelmingly enthusiastic about our chances of reaching Guduf with Norman and Claude in tow. Nor were the people who watched us pass through the rest of Ngoshe. One old boy tottered up to us, spear in hand, and almost wet himself with laughter when Waz told him what we were about to do. Donkeys had once been able to reach Guduf by way of a track up from Gwoza in the west, but the route had long since deteriorated and was now negotiable only by humans. According to the locals there had never been a way up for donkeys from where we were at Ngoshe on the eastern side. I was less impressed by this intelligence than Waz, but we paused on the outskirts of the village for a bottle of the local Coca-Cola, a refreshing preparation based on malt and pepper. It is sold in old fizzy drink bottles stoppered with strips of brown paper—special, Nigerian brown paper which is used in ever diminishing scraps for wrapping the peppered kebabs sold as snacks in every market, and in long strips to bandage new bicycles, a remarkable practice which is slowly dying out in the face of competition from lengths of coloured plastic.

Waz assessed the position. "They're pretty sure about us not making it," he said, looking pretty sure about us not making it himself. I felt that we could do it, but ignoring local advice is so much easier when you can't understand it. Unfortunately for Waz he spoka da lingo.

"Hmm," I said. There was a fly in my bottle. I tried to pour it out but it was a tremendous swimmer and I lost a good mouthful of drink for nothing. I sighed and cast my eyes unto the hills. There were extensive fields of basalt rock which would clearly defeat the donkeys, but the pink quartzites ahead of us seemed relatively gentle. Every possible square inch had been laboriously terraced, the tiny strips of soil built up over the centuries and held back by retaining walls of stone only one or two feet high. If the path was really as bad as everyone said it was we could always climb over the walls and head straight up hill. This theory actually collapsed in the face of vertical reality but I was feeling a little determined that afternoon. I had once spent an interesting couple of months with pack donkeys in the wilds of northern Kenya and I had no qualms about having a bash at the Mandaras. In any case, if I were going to abandon Norman and Claude I would rather do so in Gwoza, where I felt more confident of selling them. We would take the donkeys over the hills and down to Gwoza, even if we could not continue south with them.

The path followed the Gavva stream as it trickled down over the rocks, small patches of grass between the boulder fields giving an almost alpine flavour to the scene. I was still a little mystified as to where the water came from since the plains were dry as a bone. Norman and Claude were rather more than mystified. They were stunned. They had never in their lives experienced anything larger than a baobab tree and the mountains confounded them utterly. Perhaps the locals were right after all. Perhaps we should now turn back. If only we had brought crampons and oxygen! Never mind—be positive, press on, and we blundered forward, the donkeys reacting woodenly to our occasional assistance. They loosened up a bit in crossing the stream, which had quite sharp banks, and they took the preliminary twists of the path very well, but it was obviously going to be a physicalish afternoon.

★

159

Sweat was roaring down our bodies within two minutes of the real climb beginning. It dripped off bony eaves at elbows, chins and knees and it made little circles where it splashed on to the rocks. The loads behaved like children on a seesaw, and to relieve Norman and Claude we carried the stuff ourselves, staggering up the hillside towards Guduf in a confusion of hoof, stone and splattering brine. The path doubled among rocks juxtaposed like kissing gates with tricky drops and climbs woven in between. We worked in stages, dumping the panniers some way ahead then returning for the bewildered mokes. We panted and pushed and we heaved and we thwacked and we twisted tails and hauled on ears and ropes. We crawled under bellies which gurgled like drains and we held on tight to trembling legs, jamming them hard against the rock. At one point we had to lift Claude bodily. A jack and a large block of smelling salts would have been enormously useful. We had neither, but travellers going both ways stopped frequently and helped us out with great enthusiasm. They scrummaged round the donkeys like bees on a brood comb, nudging forward the reluctant queens. During the thickest mêlées the donkeys even laid some rather smelly eggs, luckily missing the pushers.

Waz had been silent for the first couple of miles, but as the path rose from the valley bottom he had spoken. He was probably worried in case the animals damaged themselves in the dramatic scrabble, but, whatever his motives, he was saying things that I did not wish to hear. His words only made the path a little steeper. I was committed to the hill and so I just smiled blandly, said things would be OK, and carried on. A scant half mile of mountainside was draining country which three hundred miles of plain had hardly touched. Dark stains were spreading now below the surface tangle and the underlying rock was showing through. I had already been conscious of an ordered quality to Waz's nature which was wholly lacking in the metamorphic jumble of my own; but far from blending the disparate elements of our separate beings, the exigencies of the journey were eroding them out, leaving isolated and crumbling pinnacles staring across a rapidly widening plain.

Waz became increasingly disenchanted as we worked our way up the hill, and I tried to come to terms with our differences. I was ten years older than him and a foreigner to boot. Perhaps I was just too crystallised to rub along with softer and more rounded strata, but at that moment I was not necessarily the problem. Waz was definitely out of step with himself on that hillside, but I did not know why. Maybe he was shaken by the efforts required with the donkeys. He was a fairly gentle sort of guy. I was swearing at Norman when an unexpected thought occurred. It suddenly struck me that Waz survived on harmony. I, myself, do not. To me the hill was a kind of fuel, but to him it was just waste and exhaust. As we cooked our meal that night we observed a polite distance, but we both knew that divorce was inevitable.

We had ground to a halt two-thirds of the way up to Guduf and we spread our mats on a small plot of grass beside a trickling stream. Smoke from our fire of corn stalks rose into the fading light, merging with the rocky terraces around us and with the grey-blue sky. It was cold after dark and I was a little bit sad. I was also ashamed that I had let our partnership fail. A favourite couplet passed through my mind. It was written by William Blake and although it is very short, it cuts me to the ground every time I think of it. Here it is.

> Mutual Forgiveness of each Vice,
> Such are the Gates of Paradise.

I rolled myself into a blanket, wrapped my Flooktons round a stone to take my head, and stared up at the moon. My skin felt clean as peaches but I could not sleep. I was wondering if a certain beach was restless in the moonlight, too, down on the coast of Africa. I had a fair chance of getting there, whatever Waz decided, but just then far oceans were irrelevant, and Getting seemed so unimportant in the enigmatic face of Being. In any case the moon-raked sea was not my destination, for it was with me all the time, beside me always as I ran along the shore. Sometimes a wave would catch my legs but sea-water dries so fast in all the walking, all the going and the

161

not-arriving. "Walking where?" I wondered and the geckoes sang at midnight through the rocks. "Where?" the little lizards asked. The word made walls for caves, and lids for graves, and waves rolled questionless across the night.

We woke on our first sunrise in the hills to find that sleep had done a fair job on the ravelled sleave of care. There was a slight haze in the distance, though, which indicated that the north-easterlies of the dry season had begun. These winds prevail from November through to March and squirt dust from the Sahara in densities which vary day by day, but which are sometimes thick enough to shut down airports as far south as Lagos. Cautious drivers even switch their head-lights on. The dusty wind is called the harmattan and it makes things look extremely old, behaving like a wicked fairy with a can of spray-on age. One's hair goes grey as spiders' webs and lungs produce great globs of the stuff that health inspectors dream about. The dust adds weight to every publication, investing even memoirs with the dignity of undisturbed survival. Days of thickest harmattan are also very cool because the dust absorbs and blocks a great deal of heat. On some days around New Year, which is anyway the coolest time, you even need a jersey and you feel so good between the hawking and the spitting that you may perhaps forget your grit filled eyes and your blocked-up nose.

The slight haze of early harmattan was not in actual fact the most obvious sight on that initial sunrise in the hills. What had first hit my eyeballs led me at once to the wild assumption that I was suspended from the roof of an old and much eroded cathedral, for the three faces staring down at me bore all the marks of prolonged attack by acid rain. The gargoyles spoke. They were short, squat and a severe shock to the system. They were also three parts naked, the fourth being snug inside a calabash. I wondered what they wore on Sundays and at christenings but they were jabbering nineteen to the dozen and I became engrossed in the movements of their lips. I was still in bed and so their faces appeared to be upsidedown and their chins had become grotesque foreheads. The plugs thrust through their lower lips looked just like horns and they waggled like the snouts of dropsied rhinos.

Each crone bore a headload of grain in a basket shaped like an enormous lampshade, requiring at least one hand to keep it steady. This was fortunate since the ladies were highly miffed. Considering the early hour, Waz decoded well, and he put their agitation down to corn stalks, of which we had used too many both for fodder and for fuel. We apologised and a small amount of cash changed hands. The old ladies chattered on up the trail and out of sight, their voices fading over the lip of rock which hid the Guduf Basin. Waz and I and Claude and Norman followed after we had our semovita and our vitamins.

Guduf, when we reached it, turned out to be a square kilometre or so of flattish ground, sheltered by higher peaks to the north and the south. The place would have made a superb filmset. As we crossed the lip and looked down on the widely scattered village I felt a bit like Ronald Colman trudging into Shangri La, and I half expected the Dalai Lama to pop up from behind a rock. Judging from the evidence not quite beneath my feet the lama, had there been one, might well have resented the intrusion. The ground was thick with turds. All shapes and sizes were represented, and in all consistencies, but, despite these physical variations, they were all exhibiting a most unturdlike predilection for fresh air and sunshine. They lay cool as curledup cucumbers, completely unprotected from the public gaze, and they were obviously well accustomed to this exposure. The flies swarming over them were making friends with gay abandon and brought the meningitis queue into vivid focus. Guduf was, in fact, the shittiest place that I had ever seen outside a U-bend but, as it turned out, I hadn't seen much, and the area did not retain its title of Shitsville 1980 for very long.

Tearing myself from the sordid details I looked about me. There were date palms and groves of eucalyptus trees which did a lot to freshen the atmosphere. The many baobabs had been pruned into abject servility but large fig trees and mahoganies were scattered everywhere. There were several sorts of trees with waxy leaves that I had never seen before and way above us tangled greenery was frothing on the hillsides. In fact the further up to heaven one progressed, the greener did the world become. I could make out a few compounds in the hazy distance of the terraced slopes, but here within the flatter basin the huts were loosely grouped round half a dozen minor hummocks.

The dwellings were of mud and stone, and they were most precisely thatched. The apex of each roof was drawn up into a tightly bound spike like a Prussian helmet, from which the jaw bones of cows and goats gleamed in decorative clusters. The finishing touch was provided by an upturned pot or a rusty old bowl crowning each roof point. Many many compounds had been abandoned and their walls were pouring back into the earth, revealing details of construction that I had never seen before. Unlike the standard issue hat box of adobe plus cone of thatching grass design, the huts of Guduf had solid roofs and proper ceilings. The walls were continued into a dome of mud which the thatching normally hid. The space between the apex of the dome and top of the walls was used as an attic, a floor of earth resting on branches set into the walls. Some huts had small niches in the outer walls in which sat rotund pots on stumpy legs. They were either kennels for the land crabs used as oracles throughout the hills, or else they were in the nature of shrines to ancestors of the compound head. I did not discover which.

A certain incredulity had greeted our arrival. Women were pounding grain in natural hollows of the rocks and others were piling sorghum on the huge slabs which lay conveniently about. They stopped to watch as our caravan trailed by. No donkeys, we were told, had clambered up to Guduf for at least fifteen years, and then they had come up from the west, climbing the track from Gwoza which had once been maintained by order of the district officer. This path had since deteriorated, and everything in Guduf now arrived on human heads, including all the corrugated iron for the voting booths. Most of the livestock in the district had been born there as had all the human beings other than the teachers at the primary school. In fact humans were Guduf's biggest export, which accounted for the many ruined huts. People had moved down to the plains in droves, where land was plentiful, free of stones and, blessed relief, quite flat.

"This'll do," said Waz. He had picked a shady compound, built round a group of rather comfortable rocks. We had, of course, attracted quite a crowd, largely males, many of whom were dressed in nylon swimming trunks. We unloaded all the food and had a brew, delighted at the ease with which we balanced up the cooking pot. We had only to stretch a hand for a supply of stones of any shape or size.

Having taken roughly six hours to travel less than a mile and a half, and having carried the loads ourselves for most of that time, it was obviously not a good idea to continue south through the mountains with the beasts. We were both rather pleased with ourselves for having made it up to Guduf, but our plan was now to descend the broken path to Gwoza, and there to sell our darling little donkeys. The following day was a Sunday, actually 23rd November, and by great good fortune it was Gwoza's weekly market day. We decided to continue the journey as we had started out, carrying our stuff in the rucksacks which we had so joyously discarded a month before. Waz would go back to Gulak and collect them while I was to try my luck as a salesman.

The donkeys found that going downhill was easier than going up, but they had nevertheless to be manhandled across the tricky bits. Every so often a basketful of sorghum would ascend the path, propelled by heavily foreshortened legs and a body invisible from above. A parapet of corn heads was often jammed around the rim of these baskets, thus increasing their capacity, and a simple iron sickle was invariably resting on top of the pile. We did see one or two men carrying loads up to Guduf but the major burden seemed to be on the heads of women, who were dressed in more or less the same way as the crones of early morning. Lip plugs varied in style, but the head calabashes did not, except in the number and the configuration of the cracks. The broken bits were stitched together with sutures of fibre which made some women look like victims of a bungled lobotomy. As a major concession to the mores of the plains a short piece of cloth was tied across the odd female shoulder, covering the flatter chested Gudufians to the upper thigh, but the general impression received was of utter indifference to clothes. Most people carried staves or corn stalks in their free hands to help them up the rocks.

We were ravenous, and as we crossed the two miles of flat ground between the hills and Gwoza township we gratefully accepted the peanuts offered to us by the people in the fields. We tethered the donkeys to a lorry near the market place and went into the first "hotel" that we came across. These establishments do not usually offer accommodation, but they have food on the go all day. They are generally hot and fly ridden and look a lot like the loos erected temporarily at point-to-points and summer camps. Waz and I each had a naira's worth of rice and meat, rinsing our hands in the communal dish as was the practice, and we dipped the plastic mug with its built-in quota of grime into the sunken pot for drinking water. I leant back and fell off the bench. "Hotels" always have the sort of bench that tips you off, and I never learn.

Waz crossed the road and took the first vehicle going south. He was going to spend the night in Gulak, pick up the rucksacks and meet me in the market place the following day. Meanwhile I drove Norman and Claude up to the secondary school where they spent the night chomping around in Gloria and Laurel's garden. Gloria and Laurel were surprised to see the great explorer return so soon but were most welcoming. We slung back a few ales that evening and I woke up with the taste of cockatoo shit in my mouth. The girls were still asleep. I doused the worst sensations with a hasty snack of oranges and porridge, and then the cockatoos and I drove Norman and Claude to market, where we established ourselves beneath a likely tree. It was only ten o'clock and still rather early for business. I layed out the ropes and the panniers and sat upon our ripped old sacks to wait. I had already made contact with the local government official in charge of the market. He had wished me luck and had not charged me for my pitch which I thought was nice of him. I had a super morning.

Instead of straggling around and gawping at the populace, which is what I, as a traveller, tend to do, I had the populace straggling round to gawp at me. For three hours around midday there were never less than fifty pairs of legs clustered tightly round my spot. It was like sitting in a noisy forest, with loud explanations of what I was doing being voiced from the upper branches. There were several theories, some of which Waz explained when he returned from Gulak with the rucksacks. They ranged from the familiar "Chadian refugees" theme to somewhat far fetched speculation on the European diet, and, for all I knew, on our sex lives too. To people who rarely see Europeans with animals (apart from the extraordinary affection that white people show for dogs), the sight of one actually selling stock, and in a public market too, was well worth a curious half hour.

Gwoza is a cosmopolitan sort of place with a wide spectrum of people using the market. They varied from dwarf-like creatures, down from the back of beyond with plugs in both lips and cicatrisations everywhere, to elegant Fulanis of several denominations, including a couple of Mborroro men who finally bought Claude for fifty naira. Nobody wanted Norman.

Waz tried his luck at selling while I went off to buy a couple of woven plastic sacks. They are extremely tough and light and they fold up very easily. Without the donkeys we could not carry our sleeping mats and the sacks made perfect groundsheets. Halfway through the afternoon we had a spot of light relief from the local constabulary. A couple of young policemen turned up on a bicycle whose back rest was not designed for the full weight of the law. One of them twisted the mudguard back into shape while the other asked me for my receipt.

"What receipt?" I asked. "I haven't bought anything."

They seemed incapable of understanding what a receipt was and assumed that I had stolen the donkeys. Waz did a superb job in calming the atmosphere which grew decidedly heated.

"Bring your disting," the larger constable kept saying. "Disting" is a direct translation of the Hausa phrase "abin nan" which means "this thing", hence "disting". This in turn means just about anything you want it to mean, including "er", "um", and "whatsitsname".

"I haven't got a disting," I found myself repeating. The crowd, still large, grew restive at the idiotic suspicions of the young officers who were basically out to extract a little present from myself. One old man, fed up with their behaviour, pointed to my rucksack frame. How, he asked, could Waz and I possibly be troublemakers or thieves? Bad people, he assured the crowd, do not carry their bedsteads around with them.

The law eventually cycled off with its caps arrogantly low over its eyes, but it had scared off a chap who had made several sorties in Norman's direction and had even asked the price. I would have taken more or less anything since we wanted to leave Gwoza that day and were certainly not going to wait a week for the next market day. I managed to keep a cool salesmanlike approach, however, and just about restrained myself from prayer. Waz ranged through the rapidly emptying market place looking for a buyer and the shadows lengthened. Norman looked less and less interested in life, although he brightened slightly when Gloria and Laurel dropped by with some yoghurt and a few bananas. We gave him the skins. We were about to give up when another old Fulani appeared and after bargaining not seen this side of the Chicago corn exchange I let my little friend go for five and twenty naira (about twelve pounds fifty). He had been with us for just three weeks.

16

An inconclusive but noisy scrap was in progress when Waz and I reached the uphill section of the Guduf track. Donkeyless once more, we had loaded ourselves with extra food, kissed Gloria and Laurel goodbye, and had walked back across the peanut fields to ascend and continue on our way through the hills. Forty or fifty tiddly women, also returning to Guduf, had gathered beneath the tamarinds at the bottom of the path and were encouraging the fight from ringside boulders. A few of them were performing a thoroughly uninviting striptease as they struggled from their urban glad rags into the workaday country ensemble of next to nothing or, at most, a cotton skirt gathered at the waist by elastic. One of the "artistes" fell over, but I tried not to look. The wrestlers, meanwhile, had dashed each other's calabashes to the ground and their skirts were giving way under the strain of combat. Aloof, we picked our way through a minefield of temporarily abandoned beerpots and clambered above the humming crowd. The babble floated after us, but had faded by the time we reached the stone gateway of the village.

The stuff that we had left behind (mostly rice and blankets) had been taken to the compound of Buluma Mbicha, headman of one of the village wards. We spent a couple of nights with him. His father came lurching up to the awning of mats at the entrance hut ten minutes after we arrived, with a pad of moist leaves strapped to his leg.

"What's he done?" I asked.

"He's a bit drunk," said Buluma Mbicha. He spoke Hausa.

"He wants you to look at his leg," said Waz.

I removed the leaves, revealing a very large hole in the old man's shin. He had collided with a tree stump some days before and the wound smelt bad. I dressed it and received a toothless oration of gratitude, an unsteady salute and a small pot of beer in return. That evening I also treated the oldest man in the village. He was lying under a rock, stark naked but for a green bush hat, and everything about him was ancient—his skin, his voice, his muscles, veins and genitals, and his weeping, bleary eyes. They were very sore, and Mbicha had to clamp him in a headlock so that I could get the drops in. No one really understood what the old chap was saying any more and I suppose that he wasn't far off a hole in the ground. The Gudufians used to bury people in a sitting position, wrapped in a fresh bullock hide if they were really important, but things were changing and this old boy would probably end up in a straightforward Christian or Muslim grave.

By the time I got back to the awning the beer was down to a pinkish sludge and the stars were out. Waz had replaced the lantern glass with a spare brought up from Gwoza and we sat in the glow feeling hungry, but certainly not lonely. The awning was sociably crowded and I leant back against a rock with a calabash on my head, having jokingly taken it from one of Mbicha's four wives. Hearty laughs all round. Mbicha slipped the woman some coins and she vanished through the entrance hut, returning with about two gallons of beer in a pot. It was quite normal for husbands to pay their wives for beer, indeed brewing is one of the two major sources of income for the hill women. The other is the cultivation of groundnuts. Mbicha's wife decanted a couple of pints into a small calabash and, arms interlocked, she and her husband knocked back the lot in the Siamese swig act that I had seen on my initial recce behind Madagali. I was profoundly shocked but was even more disconcerted when supper arrived and we all began to eat together from the same bowl. I had never before seen men and women eating together in West Africa and it upset my sense of decorum.

"Do they always do this?" I asked Waz.

"Sometimes," he said. "The women have much more

independence than those down people. They still do most of the work but they're more sort of individual up here. Not bad, is it?" he added, referring to the stodge of guinea corn and beans. I thought it was terrible, partly because it was cold and partly because I wanted roast potatoes and greens and fruit and ice-cream. I was getting really fed up with the local food. I told Waz.

"We'd have been eating millet if we'd come next year," he said. "They rotate it on alternate years with the guinea corn." I said that I found millet even worse than guinea corn and Waz agreed.

"It does bind you up a bit," he said, "but it's much less dangerous. Guinea corn years are deadly. It's the stubble. People are always running into the stumps, usually when they're drunk like Mbicha's father."

I had expressed an interest in the beer making process, and was consequently woken up by Mbicha's youngest wife at about three that morning. "God it's early," I thought as I stumbled after her, bouncing like a night struck pinball through the maze of separate huts. I fixed my eye upon a firelit door-way, blocked for an instant by the woman's back, and I followed her inside. Flames were bickering round three Ali Baba pots well set into the floor, and as the woman bent towards them with more wood her breasts swung forward, rich in the orange light. I watched blearily. It was certainly too early for any but the most fleeting of naughty thoughts. I propped myself against a sort of draining board set against the wall and tried to look intelligent. The dancing shadows helped and I already knew the recipe.

To make beer à la Mandara a quantity of guinea corn is first kept damp until it germinates. The sprouts are then ground with a stone on platforms like the one which was supporting me, and the resulting flour is steeped in water, boiled, and filtered through a finely woven basket. The liquid is boiled again for about five hours, a phase of the process which is crucial to the flavour. Mbicha's wife was tending the long boil as I watched, skimming off the froth as it built up in the

171

mouths of the pots. Well after sunrise, when the brew had cooled, it would be infected with natural yeast which works very fast in the heat of an African morning. The whole operation is timed to have the batch ready by early afternoon, hence the horribly anti-social working hours of a brewing day. I thanked Mbicha's wife and staggered back to bed.

We got up late, drank several pints of tea and spent the whole day up Chukume hill, the highest in the Mandaras. According to the map the summit is precisely one foot higher than Ben Nevis. The day was very hazy, like a Chinese landscape, I thought, as we tracked our way over the terraces. Isolated compounds winkled up the hillsides, each one surrounded by a fence of cactus and thorn and so integrated with the boulders that it seemed part of the natural scenery. The leather bag in which I kept my camera things was soon limp with sweat and we stopped for a drink on the forecourt of the highest compound.

"Watch your feet," said Waz as we manoeuvred round the boulders to the small verandah of beaten earth. We were about a thousand feet above Guduf and the haze was less dense. Through it we could see hills marching southward tier on tier, but, in response to Waz's warning, I refocused on a less pleasant sight. Looking down I saw that we were bridging the family dung heap. A stalagmite of human shit was mounting from the drop below. The compound was only the merest buzz away, and it was now quite obvious why epidemics lurked among the hills, especially in the wet season when all the crud washed directly into the streams. Guduf village slipped to second position on my list of unhealthy places and this hamlet of the Gavva clan shot straight to number one.

At this time of year there was very little surface water available, and so the people of the higher slopes had to go down to the wells in Guduf with their water pots, and slog all the way back uphill with fifty or sixty pounds balanced on their heads, a bit like Jack and Jill in reverse. I had once worked in an area of hills in north central Nigeria which like the Mandaras had also been a haven for the local tribes in the days

172

of slave raids. The water problem had been overcome by the construction of stone lined tanks built across fissures in the rocks, but we had not heard about similar reservoirs in the Mandaras. The impermeable rock does, however, trap water in underground hollows, some of which keep springs seeping throughout the year. The rainfall against the hills is significantly higher than on the plains, and the trees send roots slithering deep down between the rocks to search it out, hence the surprising greenery of the summits.

The ridge that we were following widened out into a series of small basins which had once been occupied and cultivated. Old hut sites were overgrown with grass and thorn, and grinding stones littered the ground. Borassus palms grew incongruously among the waxy leaved trees. The grass was still fresh and overhung the path which we eventually lost. As we threaded our way up the tangled slope we could hear the cries of women hacking at firewood in a gully below, down which poured a frozen torrent of black rocks, probably the remains of a laval intrusion into the main hill mass. Great slabs of granite had been used to bridge the gaps and heaps of stone were arranged to break the highest steps. We skipped across and approached the hilltop. The air smelt faintly of geraniums, and bamboos rustled in the breeze.

The peak itself was like an enormous playground. The hill was capped with boulders twice as big as barns, but jumbled together like children's toys at bed time. The spaces under and between the rocks were dusty dry and full of hyrax dung, the former haunt of leopards and civet cats long since hunted out. A wild tonsure of fig trees and euphorbias grew round the hilltop, knit together with a wicked, trailing thorn called *Acacia ataxacantha*. We unpicked ourselves and groped up through the maze to stand below the bare summit. Once we had found a route the actual climbing was very easy, but the exposure was magnificent.

"Fantastic," yelled Waz above the roaring wind.

Overlapping ranges were floating south like icebergs in the haze, the lower slopes diffuse upon the dusty plain. A distinct boundary hung in the sky, above which the air had lost its brownish tinge and stretched clear and blue. We grinned at each other, exhilarated, almost cold, and happy.

On the way down we passed a chap cutting grass in one of the rocky hollows on the ridge. He had prepared three bundles. The stems were finer and shorter than the plains grass, a little like the people, I thought, as we descended with the man. He was a nimble, elf-like creature, but he had a prodigious shout. It bounced across the hillsides as we passed the women who were still cutting wood down in the gully.

"They often shout," said Waz. "It saves an awful lot of walking." He laughed. "Can you imagine that there might be telephones up here one day?" he asked, but I couldn't.

We were again crowded into the lean-to and that night we had stories from Lagos. I was asking Buluma Mbicha about the various plants that we had seen and I had produced a shrivelled specimen for his examination. Waz was translating but his heart wasn't in it. Translating can be a wearisome task and it must have been difficult for him with this bearded three-year-old incessantly demanding information, but I persisted. The sprig in question was called Cock's Eye in Hausa.

"They put it into the talismans that people wear," said Waz. "They say it wards off witchcraft. Mbicha sells a lot of it in Lagos."

"But Lagos is eight hundred miles away," I said.

"Yes," said Waz. "He goes there nearly every dry season. A lot of hill men do the same thing. They collect up sacks of plants and go down there to sell them. There's a place near Dodon barracks where they sleep. Some of them even go as far as Ghana."

For supper we had lumps of steaming pumpkin with our tuwo, but we were interrupted by a bout of screeching from the darkness. Mbicha and his wives just laughed.

"It's only a girl," he said. "She's being taken to her new husband's compound. She'll shut up in a minute. It's customary for them to put up some resistance." We had been talking about chameleons, but dropped that and got on to the subject of marriage.

"It's getting ridiculously expensive," said Mbicha. "You used to exchange presents with the girl's family for years so the price got spread out, but now people make direct payments in cash. It's disgusting, just like buying something in a shop."

According to Mbicha, the going rate for a first wife was about three cows, various other presents, and about four hundred naira in cash. First marriage is an institution of very great social importance to men of the hill tribes, and is entered into by means of a complex series of gift exchanges and ceremonial family gatherings, which, in essence, provide advanced "payment" for the first two children and secure public approval for the union. This form of marriage takes place in the dry season. The year's "crop" of first marriages is celebrated publicly by the whole village at a ceremony held just before the rains, the details of which vary from place to place, although the general idea is the same.

After all the hard work necessary to obtain a first wife, it is strange that virtually all these marriages end in divorce. The convention is that a woman is free when she has "paid the bride price" by producing two or three children. She then usually wanders off to another man, often for no particular reason. The bride price for these secondary marriages is paid after the unions prove fertile, and they are not celebrated publicly. Among the Kapsiki, one of the largest of the hill tribes, women marry, on average, five times. They play a game of musical chairs with the men, hopping from place to place as the fancy takes them. The resulting children, however, stay with the father, and are supposed to be looked after by his other wives. The Kapsiki themselves admit that this arrangement is often unsatisfactory and that the instability of marriage within their society is a factor contributing to the high rate of infant mortality.

I wondered, briefly, how Waz would settle into this world of quicksilver wives, but, of course, he would never have to. The Gulak people have largely abandoned tribal practice for

Islamic law, and among the younger people there is even a trend towards monogamy.

"I'm quite lucky really," Waz had said one evening. "I mean, I can just get married how I want. If I only take one wife, people will say it's because I'm educated. If not, I can marry more than one and it's still OK. The problem is that the actual thing of it is different here than in England. Here marriage is more of a partnership and less of a relationship. We don't expect so much of the stuff like compatibility or having things in common. The main thing is being a successful husband or wife which is more to do with basics like fertility and food than with your idea of love."

Buluma Mbicha had persuaded two men to accompany us the following morning, which was nice of them because it was a busy time of year. Their names were Sadima and Lowan. Lowan carried the hurricane lamp and Sadima humped along with our sack of food. Despite the near certainty of being fed by people along the way we wanted to be independent and to have our own supplies. We only had a very rough idea of how many days it would be until we could restock. Waz and I both carried canvas rucksacks which grew whiter and whiter as successive days of sweat soaked through and left broad rings of salt in patterns on the cloth.

We roared on south from Guduf at about half a mile an hour, the snail's pace due partly to the terrain, which required scrambling over, but mostly to the frequency and duration of our halts. Lowan and Sadima stopped at nearly every compound, and while Waz and I stood around like a couple of spare beauty queens, fiddling with our rucksack straps, our guides explained our presence at great length. There had to be a reason for our walk because, first of all, it was a well known fact that all Europeans had cars, and second, the road was down below. Waz had therefore hit upon the idea of trees. We were to be studying the trees, not the actual trees where we stood but always the ones on the next range of hills. Most people seemed happy with this explanation. It was, after all, another well known fact that Europeans studied everything, which was odd since they already knew everything.

The territory of the Guduf clan ceased at a place called Baba Yaguwa, and so did Lowan and Sadima.

"They can't go on," said Waz.

"Why not?"

"They don't know the way."

"They must know it. I thought these blokes were supposed to trot all over Nigeria in the dry season. We're still only a stone's throw from Guduf."

"They do," said Waz, "they go all over the place, but they don't go this way. It's a different clan now so they've never been anywhere in the mountains beyond this hill."

Demarcation was not our only labour problem. Explaining to the guides that two hours' walk did not deserve a full day's pay was difficult, and so was the finding of replacements. The harmattan was thick enough to obscure the nearest range and without a guide we could get very lost indeed. I resorted to a dubious but successful ruse.

"Tell them they can have their money when they've found replacements for themselves," I said. Waz told them. Replacements appeared with amazing speed and we set off again, this time into the territory of the Waa which, as we soon discovered, consisted of only one hill. Our Waas ground to a halt at the frontier and we went through the guide swop routine again. The perplexing thing was that everybody still looked the same. The men were all in Oxfam jackets, raincoats and bits of clothing which, as Waz said, make them look like tramps dressed up as tramps, while the women still wore calabashes and goat skins or tiny bits of material across their shoulders. The only outward sign of changing territories were the huts which had become like mushrooms sprouting from the rocks.

Apart from my midnight foray into Mbicha's brewery I still had to explore a compound fully. It was at a place called Ufre, in Johode clan territory, that we discovered where the cows were kept. Due to irregularities of the slopes many huts rose five or six feet from base to thatch on one side, but were dug into the hillside on the other. Walking past on the uphill side of a hut in Ufre I suddenly realised that I was in imminent danger of being savaged on the knees by a cow. It was glaring from a porthole in the hut wall.

"Waz," I said, "there's a bloody cow stuck in this hut. It's standing below ground level on this side."

"It's probably a bull," said Waz, and it was.

Two days later we were following a broad but winding track across the plateau when we heard a strange rasping sound coming up fast behind us, punctuated by loud cries. Round the corner came an animal which was quite definitely a bull, and it was looking for a fight. We immediately ran away. I ended up on a rock inaccessible to all but the panic stricken and looked down. The bull was towing a large piece of wood which had been attached to its back leg as an anchor, and a man was trotting well behind that, but still in contact via a very long piece of rope. He was shouting out what was obviously the Kapsiki for, "Look out, here comes a bull."

"They usually have a bloke at the front as well as the back," said Waz, emerging from the undergrowth. "These bulls get really savage. It's not surprising. They're cooped up in those huts for two or three years and then they have to break the walls down to let them out."

Altogether we saw about half a dozen of these battery bulls trailing their owners round the mountain paths, but, despite many enquiries, no one gave me a satisfactory explanation of what they were for. I eventually found the answer in a book. The bulls are slaughtered to celebrate the new harvest at a festival held in most villages every second year. Owning such a bull brings great social prestige, and people often contribute to buy one between three or four compounds. Since it was harvest time I assumed that the bulls we saw were on their way to the ceremonies, probably taking the first and last walk of their adult lives.

We continued our zigzag progress south. The hills fell away to the east and west and when the wind died we could just hear

the swish of traffic on the Gwoza road. The insulating proper-
ties of a few miles of rock were quite extraordinary. I felt as if
I were watching two films simultaneously, the one out on the
plains a local variation of the twentieth century, but the one
around us something utterly different. A compromise had
been established on a small plateau far below us where a tin
roof was bouncing sunlight through the haze. Our Johode
guide said something to Waz.

"That's Horessa clan land," he told me. "The tin roof is a
mission school, but he is saying that nobody from here ever
goes down there."

"Down there" was less than a mile away. Although each
agglomeration of compounds could loosely be described as a
village, one felt that vertical distances of much more than a few
hundred feet produced a distinctly independent and self-reliant
attitude among the inhabitants. I have no evidence to sustain
this observation other than my feelings but it was as if every
compound were saying, "This is our place. These are the
particular rocks on which we sit, as we always have, and here
are the rocks where we dry our crops. This is where we always
grind our grain and, look, this is our view—we can see the
whole world from here."

Although he did not actually penetrate the hills, the explorer
Heinrich Barth did wind his way south within sight of them in
1851, and he had this to say of what he saw:

> A first glance at this landscape [he was just north of Gulak]
> impressed me with the conviction that I had at length arrived
> at a seat of the indigenous inhabitants. Vigorous and tall
> manly figures, girt round the loins with a short leather
> apron . . . seemed to intimate that this ground belonged to
> them, and that the foreigner, whoever he might be, ought
> to act discreetly.

Towards the evening of our first rucksacking day the hills
grew more subdued. We were approaching the plateau which
runs into the Cameroons and we stopped beside a stream to

have a wash. The path was obvious and our guide, the Buluma of Kolika clan, just pointed up the hill. Two women scuttled by. For some reason they reminded me of the White Rabbit in *Alice in Wonderland*. They both had full loads of sorghum on their heads and one had a baby slung in a goatskin on her hip. We hurried after them, climbing the broken track to the village of Ngossi. The headman's name was Mahadi Gdula, a slight but handsome man of about forty-five, dressed in a blue jersey and white bell-bottoms with a Mediterranean flavour about them. His radio was tinkling away beside him as he sat in the evening air.

"Ose!" he said, which was a generally used welcome.

"Jam na," we said, which was an equally well used reply. I never did find out what it meant, but it worked. Mahadi Gdula brought us water as we lay across the roots of the acacia tree which overhung his compound. The air was beautifully cool and I slipped into a thin jersey and long trousers.

Mahadi had five wives, an enormous woodpile and about a dozen goats. His huts looked like a group of tipsy witches gathered over sherry. There were seventeen of them, one leading straight into another, like a house whose individual rooms join up despite having separate roofs. I stooped into the first hut which was Mahadi's own. It was about two big steps across and contained a sprung bed on blue legs and several showers of clothes cascading from wonky pegs. Receding into the gloom were other openings, one inside the other. I was looking straight through the next three huts and although the whole compound was less than fifteen yards across, being in it was a confusing experience. None of the huts had windows, and so it got darker and darker as we progressed. I stumbled over several goats and skinned my legs before I went back for the torch, which revealed little attics where dried beans and nuts were stored, and great, adobe walled silos of grain rising from floor to ceiling in two of the central huts. I saw an old shield and several spears tucked beside the roof poles, but, all in all, the place was pretty bare. Each wife had her own sleeping room, with great slabs of acacia for beds, and the brewing places were similar to those which I had seen in Guduf. In addition to goats and chickens, Mahadi also had a bull. The sunken floor of its stall allowed its nose to poke out at ground level, within range of a stone water trough and loose strands of the hay which had been dropped on its way through the porthole.

The very limited space between the huts was stiff with poking out bits of thatch and broken pottery, but goats and children zoomed excitedly about the maze, with me blundering like a clumsy ferret behind them. The gaps between the outer huts were blocked with stones and adobe, making the complex very difficult to penetrate. Although the whole compound looked several thousand years old, Mahadi had built it only ten years before, when he had hived off from his father and brothers. It had taken him five weeks to build it, with the help of his relatives who were dotted about the countryside in their own little clusters.

A dense growth of corn stalks had been sickled off at the knee and the surrounding fields were bristling like hedgehogs in the moonlight. I asked why the crop seemed so much thicker than in other places.

"Fertiliser," Mahadi said. "They don't use it in Guduf, God knows why not, but here I personally collect the money and we get it up from Madagali." The Nigerian government heavily subsidises nitrates which are now available in most parts of the country, and it often falls upon men like Mahadi to arrange for the final distribution. He spent most of the evening on the opposite hillside nagging at his relatives to cough up for the supplies that they had used during the season. Supper was consequently a cliff hanger. It was always rather embarrassing when food did not appear. One could never actually ask if one was going to be fed as this would be to imply that one expected it, but if, as sometimes happened, we began to cook, a bowl of food would invariably arrive. The evening meal is taken in most of Nigeria just after sunset, but here in the hills people did not eat until much later. Mahadi returned with handfuls of money at about nine o'clock and a small pot of tuwo and beans was put before us, not a great deal for all the wives, babies, younger elements, Mahadi and ourselves, but luckily this was just the hors d'oeuvre. The main course was taken in liquid form and consisted of roughly five gallons of beer. Everyone, including the babies, had their turn at the calabash. A certain amount of Siamese drinking went on and consequently my jersey was soaked.

"Beer is really important to these people," said Waz. "I reckon it probably makes up a quarter to a third of their food intake. It's not like getting drunk, it's just a nice way of eating guinea corn."

Mahadi was a very easy chap to be with and was quite interested in our journey. He had never been up to Guduf, that not being his country, but he had travelled widely in Nigeria and the Cameroons. He told us that the Guduf people, like his own, originally came from Tulu, about two miles south of us on the Cameroonian border where a prominent rock formation stuck out above the plateau. From Tulu, he said, a rough vehicle track eventually plugged into the Cameroonian road system. Mahadi turned the radio down.

"The old people round here know all the old people who live in Guduf because they all came from Tulu together." By "old people" I think he meant ancestors several generations past. "Now we even speak different languages, but we all began in the same way," he said, and proceeded to tell us how it happened.

"There were two brothers and a sister. The senior brother had a flock of sheep and every morning he sent the younger brother and sister out to the bush to look after them. They got bored with this and one day they decided that they wouldn't do it any more. Then the younger brother saw his sister's vagina. He thought it was a wound and he bandaged it up, but it never got better. Then one day something got into the boy's head and he took away the bandage and he slept with her. He saw signs of her pregnancy and he was afraid so he went back to his senior brother and told him about his sister's stomach, thus revealing the incest. The senior brother sent his sister and his junior brother away and they started their own family and that is how the Tur and the Guduf people began."

A boy called Umaru helped us with our loads as far as Tulu, where he became distinctly agitated and wanted to go home. Echelons of young people were strung along the track with empty baskets and walking sticks of sugar cane. They were heading for the fields and did not want to play at being porters. We split Umaru's load and floated through the village, relieved to find it almost deserted and without a customs post. The track was crunchy underfoot, the hillside rock a rotten pink which crumbled into little cubes, each faced with glassy mica. The soil was poor and very thin—simply a place for the plants to put their shoes while praying to the sun, but as we plodded on, the plateau slowly opened out and began to look more fertile. I became aware of a man's voice shouting from a wide dip in the landscape to the west. Waz thought that he was announcing a death, which he was. Drumbeats rolled out through the broken grass, a mourning undertow of song developing between the strokes. A mile of empty bush divorced us from the sad reality and we continued over the widening land, the doumba, doumba, doumba dum for company. It did not go on for long which meant that the death was probably that of a baby.

We dozed off in the haze at the side of the track. An eagle swung off a rock and an old woman came by, coughing a veined dug from her shirt as she went. A lizard ran across my chest and for some strange reason a chameleon was trying to dig a hole in the middle of the road. The stream beside us had dried to a trickle between rock bound pools, and in the next one that we came to was a turtle, something between an ashtray and a saucer in diameter. It must have jumped like a salmon to get up there. Five miles later we reached Visik where I had been before.

Usman of the white raincoat was out, but a few hundred yards before his compound we had seen a covey of women harvesting a field. They were in the traditional state of undress,

183

of which I wanted photographs, but I was sure that they would vanish at the merest twitch of a camera. The problem was neatly solved by their husband who, seeing us go by, had followed. His name was Dlimo and there was a medical crisis. We went back across the fields, I with the first aid kit and Waz with the camera gear. Dlimo had a very sick daughter. She was eighteen years old and weighed about five stone, but I do not know what was wrong with her. I listened to a description of the symptoms which was couched in the normal way. She was "hot inside", felt sick and didn't eat. I hadn't a clue, left some pills and suggested the nearest hospital. No doubt she died at home. I was getting callous, or perhaps just a little less European in my approach to illness. Dlimo's young son was much easier to deal with. He had run into a corn stalk and had a septic middle toe. It was wrapped in leaves in the usual way, which kept the flies out and the germs in. We sat on a mat outside the compound, the boy in Dlimo's lap, while I cleaned the wound. My patient's name was Umaru, the second of the day, and he was a stoic, being far more interested in Waz and the camera than in the pain.

The wives had appeared and under the pretext of snapping me Waz got a few good shots of traditional Vomengu dress. It seemed to consist of two items, viz., a leather waist band from which leaves were hung to the rear and kneelength leather tassels to the fore, and, from another band, a bundle of what looked like six-inch tent pegs protecting the tassels and much else no doubt. The French call the tent-peg arrangement a "cache-sex". The wives had beads and amulets round their necks, and their skin was a beautiful ochre colour because they had anointed themselves with a mixture of mahogany oil and clay. They looked extraordinarily fine.

Dlimo was very grateful for our services. We nibbled peanuts and drank tea with him. He had twelve children altogether and five wives, but both figures had fluctuated over the years.

"You Europeans only have one wife, isn't that so?" he asked.

"Yes," I said, "only one at a time, anyway."

He thought about this for a while. "But what would you do with more than one?" he reflected. "You don't make farms. We people here need them for farming."

Umaru's smart white bandage had attracted onlookers. Among his admirers was a boy of five with very long gingery hair. Dlimo explained that the boy's mother had not become pregnant again since his birth and he would remain shaggy until she did. His head would then be shaved and they would brew lots of beer and kill a goat. Waz had struck up a friendship with the boy who was smearing sticks with a gummy substance in order to trap small birds. Meanwhile a dog had begun to sniff around my feet.

"He looks quite like you, Steve," said Waz.

"Thanks a lot," I said.

"What's his name?" Waz asked Dlimo.

"Giddere," he said.

"What does it mean?" I asked. Waz again conferred with Dlimo.

"It means 'A Heap of Rubbish'."

"Do they always give dogs names like that?" I asked.

"Gar! No, sorry, I'm talking about this boy with the ginger hair. His mother's babies kept dying so when he was born they put him outside for everyone to see, you know, just like a heap of rubbish."

We ploughed through a bowl of sweet potatoes and then went back to Usman's compound. He turned up just before dark, still in his raincoat, with a stick of green bananas strapped to his bicycle. I think he was quite surprised to see me.

I stubbed my toe while defecating in the night and the niggling sore annoyed me for the first hour's walk across the bush to Mabas. We stopped beneath the fig tree and, although it was only nine o'clock, we had our elevenses. We did not really want to leave the cavernous shade of the fig. Many of the dangling roots had coalesced. They looked like the props that Salvador Dali puts in some of his paintings.

The plateau rolled on behind the screen of fig and so, eventually, did we. The land dipped and swooped to distant hills, dropping in the east to Mokolo and rising on our right to several exposed massifs, including the one on which I had lost my map seven weeks before. Beyond it lay the isolated table land of Sukur. Red and purple grasses shimmered on the breeze and small herds of cattle moved like flecks of marble in the scrub. Waz had a blue handkerchief around his head and when he stopped he looked like a cornflower squatting in the bushes. I was doing a certain amount of squatting too, which I was used to, but I had been lately seized with stomach cramps and I hoped that they would soon go away.

Eight miles south of Mabas we saw a wondrous sight. The sky was fairly clear and at a distance on the smoky flats we saw the peaks of Mogode. They were the hills of fairy land, the ultimate in phalli and Waz called them the Rockosaurs, which they might well have been, for from our vantage point they looked like open-air exhibits of reptilian proportions. We could have been looking on the land of Mordor, modelled by a Texan, and we were going to pass straight through it.

Waz had a relative in the area and we tracked her down to the only compound remaining at a place called Yele. The huts were simple beehive shelters of mats and saplings, with a cleared space marked out like a small parade ground for praying, and Muslim robes and kettles and no beer at all. The relative had once been married to Waz's grandfather, but was now the wife of a crotchety old Fulani. She was a Fulani herself and had not seen Waz since he was eight, but she knew all about his adventures in England. Being a Fulani, the husband's source of income was chewing the cud in close proximity, and the air around the compound was soupy black with flies. Despite the distraction we managed to enjoy the sunset.

Five ground hornbills were pobbling around among the bushes not too far away. They are large, black birds with a well developed but depressing graveside manner and enormous beaks. Toward the north, the Mandaras were glowing like ripe wheat. A tiny breeze dried sweat, disturbed the flies, and brought with it the solo piping of a herdboy, chicken sounds, the grunts of men in prayer and of women at their cooking fires. Insect noises rose from the darkening grass and still in the air behind us were the entities of rock, the Moongates that had cast us spellbound earlier in the day. Actually they were nothing of the sort, being simply volcanic plugs of which there are plenty in central France, but they did do powerful things to the imagination. We were given a soup of sorrel leaves and peanuts by Waz's relative who looked quite pleased to see him. In the night I had dreadful belches and a protracted spell beyond the sleeping cows. The stars were wonderfully clear but I had run out of paper.

We were keen to explore a Rockosaur, but the husband of Waz's relative decided that we should seek permission first. We agreed because many of them were sacred and we did not want to trespass. The husband led us four miles south to Mogode, the largest village in the district, Fulani and Muslim by culture although originally Kapsiki. It was on our route in any case.

I was feeling lousy as we entered the village. A lot of pious old men were sitting outside the mudwalled gateway to the laimido's house. "Laimido" is a Fulani word for headman. The defeat of the Fulani by the British and the French left something of a power vacuum in the hills because the fragmented tribes could not be left to run themselves peacefully. Tame Fulanis were therefore re-installed as district headmen by the colonial powers, which is why their Muslim culture has gradually replaced the traditional Kapsiki way of life.

Our host disappeared into the gateway and we waited for half an hour. A government Land-Rover rolled up and a youngish chap in denims and desert boots got out. Needless to say he had sunglasses and a briefcase. Waz was told that he was the local politico, the Cameroons being a one party state. Before I left England I had read a book called *Gaullist Africa* which presents evidence of some South African-style goings on in the internal security building in Yaounde, the capital.

There is, apparently, a room in the building nicknamed the "chapel" where the gendarmes "often from North Cameroon, especially chosen for their cruelty" hold "services". These consist of beating people to death in a variety of nasty ways. We did not expect to be bludgeoned to a pulp but there was a distinct atmosphere of tension in Mogode, apparent to both Waz and I, and so we just got up and left, and kept on walking south. I ducked into the bushes every time a car went past and on one of these diversions I collided with a leper. He had a bundle and a limp, but no nostrils. He spoke a bit of French, and all three of us walked down the road together until we reached a place called Gouria. The leper was looking for a certain man with healing powers, but Waz and I just wanted an "hotel".

We felt hungry and lethargic and swarmed about a local youth who had been lounging by the roadside. His name was Michel Zra. He was roughly five foot nine, made beanpoles look overweight and, despite the heat, was wearing a thick, white, knitted cap whose tassel hung between his shoulder blades. His faded jeans were widely flared and swished with every step. There was, he said, a nearby bloke who sold soft drinks from a cool water pot but if we wanted food his cousin was our man.

"Il est chef," said Michel, who had attended the primary school in Mogode for some years. "On trouve beaucoup de Blancs ici. Ils aiment les pinnacles et les massifs."

The Rockosaurs were famous, and attracted a steady trickle of Blancs who would pass through Gouria on their way to the tourist facility at Roumsiki, five miles down the road. Michel's job was to divert them to his cousin's establishment, some two hundred yards off the highway. Michel's cousin was called Martin Teri. The trickle of Blancs was not quite steady enough to keep his cooking fire going all the time and a shower of ash and sparks blew from the doorway of his kitchen hut as he fanned the charcoal oven.

"Je vais preparer le riz," he said, "ou bien peut-être vous préférez les pommes de terre?" We ordered both. Martin was

so solicitous, so concerned for our welfare that at first I suspected trouble, but I eventually relaxed. He was a superb host
and should have been working in Paris. Even Waz was moved
to comment when we were asked if we wanted coffee before
or after the meal.

"You can see these people never lived under the British," he
said.

The rice was dehusked by a small boy and winnowed on the
light air. Michel had removed his maroon jersey, but retained
the cap. I noticed that he had a scanty beard. He was tuning a
Kapsiki harp and gave us "Au Claire de la Lune" as we drank
the coffee.

"Voilà, Michel, le musicien," said Martin. "Il invite les gens
ici à la maison." Martin had actually cleared a track so that
vehicles could bump right up to his compound. He knew what
Europeans liked. "Ici vous avez la vérité Africaine," he said.
"Tout est véritable. Là-bâs à Roumsiki, c'est pour le touriste,
mais ici ils peuvent se mettre sur les roches."

Martin also ran a music business. His grandfather had taught
him how to make most of the instruments used by the Kapsiki,
which were actually very similar to those of neighbouring
peoples. The materials of construction were small calabashes
and bent sticks, stretched reptile skins and pieces of tin cans,
the products being mostly simple harps and small guitars.
Martin also made bamboo flutes, but not drums. As a sideline
he dealt in the carvings and the brasswork for which the hill
smiths are well known. On the dusty walls of his sleeping hut
were curling polaroids of customers who had long since flown
away.

There are certain sorts of wasp in Africa which build igloos of
mud on the walls of peoples' houses, droning in and out with
hods of goo clamped in their mouths. The larvae eventually
burst out in a shower of dried earth, leaving a miniature
archaeological ruin in their wake. The wasps will also build on
curtains, picture frames and furniture. There were even red
foundations building up on the bundle of letters which Martin

took from his table. They were written on airmail paper, most of them posted in Germany, and they said how nice it was to have been in the Cameroon and if he ever got to Germany he could always stay and so on. There are certain things that I cannot explain and so I just left Martin nattering with Waz. In the meantime I engaged Michel.

17

The Rockosaurs had lovely names and Michel called them out as we passed by. Mzarmba and Dilili stood on the very edge of the plateau, dropping sheer into a deeply bitten valley at whose head stood Roumsiki and the "campement" for visitors. We each had a lemonade, sold in bottles with the lever action stoppers still commonly used in France. The shadows of Zevou and Zivi had started to move out across the plain like trickles of dark honey, and so we left our empty bottles on the bar and put the road behind us.

Apart from a short diversion into Mubi, we used only footpaths for the next hundred miles.

We followed Michel westwards along the path which led back into Nigeria, and we spent the night with a relative of his in the village of Sina Gali. Waz was more or less back on home ground again because we were now out of Kapsiki territory and among the eastern branch of his own tribe. The architecture was distinctly different from anything that I had seen before and is, I later discovered, unique in Nigeria. We were to see what is the best example of this style when we reached the village of Futude the following evening.

I woke before dawn. A dog had barked persistently throughout the night, and I had been dimly aware of Michel as he rose to stone the cur from time to time. The moon was still blazing clean through the constellation of Leo, reducing the usually rampant stars to a faint mew, but it was dark enough to see Orion doing a Fosbury Flop over the western horizon. Venus and Mars were now well separated, an indication of the weeks that had passed since the first sunrise of our walk, when, with Jupiter, they had formed a tight cluster in the eastern sky.

We walked all morning over grassy hills which reminded me of the Cheviots, except that it was hotter. There were no trees but stubby clumps of a plant called *Euphorbia poissoni* broke through the grass from time to time. They looked like the blunt, grey antlers of a herd of misplaced reindeer. Euphorbias are the African version of cacti, which do not occur naturally on the continent. Hedges of another euphorbia, *Euphorbia deightonii*, were growing round the few compounds that we passed. The cows we saw were tiny, and European in shape, and the goats were minute too. They looked like terriers and had high pitched bleats.

Although walking has distinct disadvantages, it seems to be the sort of lowest common denominator among the various ways of travelling, from which perhaps springs the proletarian camaraderie of the footpath. *The Canterbury Tales* could not have been written from the back of a Cortina, nor from a Rolls-Royce come to that. There is, moreover, a distinction to be made between the European walker who is more often than not doing it for fun, and the rest, who do it because they have to. I once attended a party in the Sierra Nevada de Santa Marta, a group of mountains which are being slowly washed out of the Colombian province of Magadalena and into the Caribbean Sea. The guests were all raw toothed peasants with smallholdings on the eroded mountain sides. They had to climb for miles in the wellies that they seemed to favour, swinging along with their jars of rum and their machetes to reach the host's crude hut. Having danced themselves silly to the music of an accordion, and, of course, having finished off the rum, they all walked home again, singing loudly and shouting to each other as they went. There was no competitive revving up of cars, no last bus to catch, nor any righteous padding home on foot because it does you good. Everyone just walked. The party remained in my memory not only for the fun but for the feeling, which I can only describe as "rightness", that accompanied the walking there and back. I have experienced the same feeling on many foot journeys since, but it came back particularly strongly among the hills in which we now found ourselves, probably because there were no alternative forms of transport.

A man called Jam caught us up early in the morning. He was suffering badly from verbal diarrhoea, or perhaps it was dysentery, because he managed to talk non-stop for five hours, which is how long it took us to reach Futude. Even the steep bits did not shut him up. He looked like an imp who had somehow slipped past his fortieth birthday. He had a bagful of honey on his shoulder and a few bits of kola nut stashed in his bonnet, a nondescript rag which looked more like a sock than a hat, but he did at least know the way.

Grass grew tall in the gullies and about three miles short of Futude we stopped for a drink where the track crossed an overgrown stream. We were about to set off again when we heard someone coming up behind us, so we waited, and from the bushes stepped the Maiden of the Mandaras. My eyeballs nearly popped right out. She rang so many bells, made so many neurones tingle, that I was reduced to photographs and saved my thoughts for later. And it wasn't lust, at all. She was actually quite ugly, but a potent symbol, the more powerful for being so utterly simple. What hit me was the colour, the deep copper of her skin and of the leather sling and the woven crib that she carried on her back. And then her movements, graceful and unhurried as giraffes, and, closer, the smile of a recent birth. The baby was three weeks old, she said.

"She's beautiful," said Waz, as we walked along together, "but I don't know why. I think it's because she's so sort of natural, all there, if you see what I mean. She makes you feel a bit excessive and unnecessary, doesn't she?"

The Maiden had nothing on except a strip of leather which was tucked between her thighs, a bracelet on each wrist, and a belt of metal beads. The crib was finished off in decorated tassels which bounced against her hips, and running up her belly to the shadow of her breasts were rows of tiny scars. She also had cuts upon her cheekbones and her chin, and her head had been shaved quite recently. She was about nineteen or twenty years old (the child was her third), and she was married to a man of over sixty. He lived in Futude and he happened to be Michel's maternal grandfather, which meant the Maiden was his granny.

There were some very unusual things about Futude. It stood on the flattened summit of the Ndille Hills at just over four thousand feet above sea level, and it was the highest village in the district. Surrounding the houses were small pastures fenced with stock proof hedges of spiny euphorbia and stone, and inside the fields more tiny cattle grazed. They were the size of Jersey heifers, but black or chocolate brown in colour. A fair cross section of the population was bashing out its laundry on the rocks and a flower bed of washing had blossomed out to dry beside a stream we had to cross before the final pull up to the houses. The compounds were separated by stonepaved alleyways with dry-stone walls built up on either side. Such permanence in rural West Africa I had never seen before. Each group of huts was approached through a walled courtyard with great piles of firewood heaped on wooden platforms running round the sides.

A matronly figure in a thin green jersey waddled round us with a basketful of guavas and lots of sympathy. We had entered the compound of Michel's oldest brother, Dauda, a man of middle age. They shared the same father but had different mothers. Dauda was in Michika but would be back that evening, and in the meantime his old aunt was making us welcome. Our gear had been taken from the courtyard, carried through the entrance hut and dumped into the sleeping quarters which were unlocked for our use. I noticed that all the huts had locks on them which struck me as rather odd since there was nothing much to steal. Locks were, in fact, one of the first items of European manufacture that the Kapsikis adopted, an interesting reflection on the importance that Kapsiki people place on self-sufficiency and privacy.

Futude had a church and a diesel driven flour mill, helicoptered up by the army some years before. There were some graves near the church, finished off in cement, but the old, pagan burial ground was overgrown and hardly used. The tombs were dug into the steep little slope and marked by low towers of stone, each with an upright slab jutting like a spire from the top. We sat on Futude's answer to Boot Hill and drank in the sunset, watching a group of swallows bouncing like specks of ash above the panoramic drop into the plains. A bone white footpath lay below us, bare as a dead snake's spine, zigzagging down the hillside till it vanished in the haze. It was a peaceful scene. Waz announced his resignation just as the hill shadow touched a distant Rockosaur.

"I've decided it's enough," he said. I lit a cigarette. I felt relieved and ashamed at the same time. The strain of an uneasy partnership would be gone, but, although he was too gentlemanly to point them out, Waz's declaration brought home a few unpalatable truths about myself. I said something like "fair enough" or "right oh", and we settled the details. He would come with me as far as the River Benue, about ten more walking days away, which would give Michel a chance to adjust himself to the journey. I had only hired Michel for a couple of days at the rate of three naira plus food a day, but he seemed genuinely keen to go on.

"If you weren't on foot like this I would not accept only three naira," he said when I had asked him to continue. Perhaps he meant that since I was obviously so poor as to be walking he was giving me a discount. We had a language problem. It was simply that, although we spoke eight different languages between us, we did not have one in common. I spoke English with Waziri and French with Michel, while they skipped from Fulani to Kapsiki between themselves. Waz knew a bit of Spanish and was for ever adapting phrases like "Como va hombre?" into what he thought might be French, but these were conversion jobs rather than translations and they didn't really work.

The people of Futude had a habit which I had never before encountered in bush villages and one of which I thoroughly approved. They took hot baths. We were each presented with a bucket of steaming water on our return from the cemetery and we sloshed about happily in the cool night air. I felt immensely refreshed as we sat toasting ourselves round the firepit while Dauda cooked a chicken. The old aunt sat with us, too, scolding the fleets of children who passed through and occasionally giving directions to her nephew; a very unusual state of affairs, I thought. Women's lib had crept into some unexpected places. She was still forcing guavas down our throats but had put a calabash over the silver grizzle on her head. It was my big chance to investigate the phenomenon and I asked Dauda why the women seemed to be so keen on their wooden head gear.

"God knows," he said. "It's just the way they've always been. They get arrested if they wear them down in Mokolo, but it doesn't stop them."

"Why do they get arrested?" I asked.

"The Cameroon side don't like us to be as we were," said Dauda, "so the police make the women wear cloth wrappers and take off the calabashes."

The garrulous Jam turned up at eight o'clock and talked of hunting at some length, in fact it was precisely the length which it took to serve up the chicken. We all knew that he was bluffing because hunting was a subject about which he knew absolutely nothing, the wildlife having run away or died when he was still a child. He had spent the afternoon with a bottle of palm wine, obtained down in Michika from southern Nigerians who Jam described as "Les Types Européens". Michika was full of them, he said, and, as for Yola, there were palm trees crawling with "types" as far as the eye could see. He was getting a bit muddled up, but it is true that palm wine is more widespread as a drink south of the Benue than in the north.

It took two more days and a short tractor ride for us to reach the town of Mubi, where we had a rest. My insides had started to bother me. The trots were just a normal part of daily life and caused no great alarm, but I was now having to nip behind the rocks after every meal and often in the night. I was seized by a discomforting cramp on the descent from Futude which was not eased by the switchback path. The countryside had grown very complicated. Valleys seemed to spring off in all directions, and were blocked by a wearisome steeplechase of tree studded ridges over which we had to make our way.

We left Futude on a Sunday, exactly a week after the Gwoza market episode, and found ourselves purchasing bananas in the back of beyond by mid-morning. A few men were standing outside a church with Bibles in their hands. They wore heavy corduroy jackets, leather shoes, and enormous kipper ties. The women were mostly in leaves and looked more comfortable. The village tamarinds were hung with yellow cobs of maize and Waz bought some for us to munch with the bananas.

Squirrelling our way through country choked with trees and boulders, we kept our ears open for the locals, who were rare and shy. We would occasionally hear the thud of threshing flails and looking up we would sometimes catch a glimpse of coppery bodies flitting out of sight. Around about Sunday lunch time, as I was dreaming of what I might have had to eat in other circumstances, we hauled ourselves into the village of Lague, population one. Everybody else was out. I was feeling wonky and sat gratefully against a wood pile. Waz and Michel went to fetch some water and they came back with the inhabitant. She was in her thirties. Being slightly lost we grilled her intensively but she didn't know the way to anywhere, having never left the tiny valley, or so she said. I began to despair of ever leaving it myself, but felt better for a brew and jolted down behind the others to a place called Za Girta. It was nothing much more than an open river bed with a few compounds flung against the neighbouring hillside. A dozen traders dribbled in as we were preparing a meal, and they opened their battered cardboard boxes in the shade of a large baobab tree. There was not much for sale, just a few sweets, some matches and soap, sunglasses, batteries, and a scent that smelt of all the brothels in the world. I bought some, God knows why.

Michel wrote a letter to his wife, saying that he would not be home that afternoon as expected, and he gave it to a trader to pass on. Waz bargained for some sugar cane and the local boyos came to stare at us. Waz translated a few of their comments.

"They're probably travelling," one of them said of us. "These whites can go anywhere. If there's a bank they can just go straight in and get money. The bank just gives it to them."

"They don't even mind if you abuse them," said another.

"Just try it," said the chap who knew about banks, "you'll sleep in Michika prison. They beat the wire and the EnPees come to get you." "Beat the wire" is the way telephoning is expressed in Hausa, and EnPee stands for Nigeria Police.

We continued, our minds in neutral and our stomachs full of rice and tea. We usually walked in single file, and that afternoon I mesmerised myself with the tassel of Michel's white hat swinging along in front of me. It suddenly shot straight into the air. Its owner, I noticed, had left the path at speed. A gibbering maniac was screeching up the track towards us, slashing at the undergrowth with vicious swipes of his machete. When a second bush whacker appeared, also in a cloud of severed vegetation, I jettisoned my rucksack and edged towards the nearest rock.

"It's OK," said Waz, looking a little startled, "here come the rest." A dozen boys were prancing up behind the whirling scouts. They were wound in vivid turbans, with ostrich plumes in screaming colours tucked into the cloth. A drummer was beating time. Green and orange tassels bounced across their shoulders as they moved, and round their waists were dozens of brass bells attached to leather belts. They whizzed around their drummer like rabid birds of paradise, then passed on down the track as suddenly as they had come.

"What was that in aid of?" I asked.

"They're just playing," said Michel, "going down to Za Girta to amuse themselves. People give them money when they dance like that, then they can buy themselves some beer. It's just young boys that do it mostly."

We crossed a gravelly stream and stopped to take a bath. The water was almost cold. I had just clambered back into my shorts when an old and naked crone appeared. Chewing her gums she squatted at the water's edge and began to wash a calabash of beans. We were hardly more than two feet apart, the water trickling between us, and so I naturally gave her a hand, pouring the beans from one bowl to another and chucking out the ones that seemed to float. Waz explained that these were the ones with weevils in them. The old lady hadn't seemed to notice that I was white, in fact I could have been a Martian for all the curiosity she showed. She tore off a handful of leaves to replace the withered bunches hanging from her waist, and disappeared.

The courtyard in which we slept that night belonged to a man called Arnado. He had three wives, one of whom was in Mubi hospital. Arnado was into bees and his compound was full of newly finished hives, cone shaped objects made of woven grass and waterproofed with dung. The hives were closed off at the base and a plug of dried dung and straw was jammed into the pointed end, with a tiny hole for the bees to use. They would soon be dotted above the surrounding countryside, tied into the branches of suitable trees and left until Arnado thought that a crop might be ready. The plugs would then be removed and the honeycomb extracted, the bees having been stupefied by torches of smoking grass. Speaking from personal experience of honey gathering in the Bamenda Highlands, I feel bound to report that torches of smoking grass do not always work and you can end up quite badly swollen. I had woken up on the morning after my first try looking like a Michelin Man, minus the smile.

I hit my head on a projecting piece of bark when I got up for my nocturnal session in the rocks and thereby learnt an interesting fact. The wood pile was marked off into separate sections for each wife so that there would be no arguments as to whose fuel was whose and in the morning Arnado was most insistent that the bark went back exactly where I had knocked it out.

We crossed the headwaters of a stream called Pokoti, dropping a thousand feet into a basin of rolling grass and occasional trees, beneath one of which an old man was sitting, picking out the seeds from an enormous pile of cotton. Two little boys were helping him. At home in England the children would be opening their Advent calendars and hurrying on the days till stocking time. It was December 1st.

The character of the hills had changed. They were now like enormous city blocks, with the streams cutting at right angles in between them. We noticed isolated women sprinkled about the landscape. The sight was almost surrealistic, little brown dots squatting on their haunches and scratching at the silent earth with their digging sticks. They were harvesting a kind of sedge called *Cyperus esculentus*, otherwise known as the tiger nut or the earth almond. To me it looked like couch grass. The rhizomes taste of marzipan and are eaten either raw or roasted on a metal sheet. We startled a little girl as we walked past. Hitching up the baby in her charge she ran across the open ground towards the nearest adult, of which she was an exact model, right down to the leaves. The one slight problem was that leaves are leaves and do not come in children's sizes after early spring. This made the little girl's clump a bit too bulky and it got caught up round her knees.

We had been told by various people of a smith who lived in the village of Tumbicha, which is where we found ourselves at midday. The people there were Falis, recognisable by three lines of cicatrisations running across their foreheads. The Higis and Kapsikis have their marks cut at the corners of their mouths. The smith's name was Buba, and although his wife was out he gave us lunch, which first required the excavation of a plant I knew as the mountain yam. Its spindly vine belies the depth at which the vegetable grows.

Buba's workshop was much the same as any other hut, but all the space inside was taken up by tools and a simple furnace. Long handled tongs emerged from querns brim full of gritty water and bits of iron scrap were littered on the floor. Pumping the bellows looked quite easy, indeed an uncircumcised boy of six was at it, forcing air in rhythmic bursts from a pair of goatskin bags and down a long clay tube whose snout was tucked into a nest of red hot charcoal. Wings of violet flame shimmered over a glowing hoe head on which Buba had been working. I asked to have a go. The trick was to nip off the opening in the bags with a smart flick of the wrist just before each stroke. Squatting down eagerly, I pumped as hard as I could, but completely forgot about the nipping. The left hand bellow immediately expired and a cloud of dust flew up from the right. I fell over, the boy resumed his place, and the hoe head began to glow again.

Buba ducked into the entrance at a shout from the boy. His movements within the workshop suggested near infallibility. The stone on which he sat had almost jumped into his hand, and even his spittle seemed to know exactly where it was going. He hardly looked at the fire, but muttered something to the boy, who ceased to pump and, taking a pair of tongs, he withdrew the hoe. He hit it very little but seemed satisfied and thrust it into the water with a squelch. Over the yam he showed us some of the brass things he had made. He used the widespread "lost wax" method of casting in which a wax model is encased in clay, leaving a small hole through which the molten brass is poured once the clay is hard. The wax evaporates and is displaced by the metal, and when it has set the clay mould is simply broken off. I bought a small pipe bowl.

Buba put us on the southward trail and we slogged forward another five miles, resting at a village called Baagira. It was tucked beneath a stupendous cliff of granite, an inselberg which rose sheer for fifteen hundred feet. White bellied storks were sailing into space from an awesome overhang which is still waiting for an enterprising climber.

It was getting hotter by the minute and we had walked too far that day, but were determined to reach a place called Duda, twelve miles east of Mubi. We had decided on a short diversion. Waz had relatives in Mubi with whom we could rest, and there was a motorable track leading from Duda into the town. We hoped that we would get a lift. Singing "the Kemptown race track's five miles long, Doo-dah! Doo-Dah!", we ground into the last three miles which were a drag, except that we met a man who tried to sell us a dead cane rat. He swung it by the tail like a rodent conker, claiming to have just that moment clubbed it on the head. It was a ferocious looking beast with long yellow teeth and nasty curled up hands, a real grand-daddy rat which the man had probably found dying in the hedge. Cane rat tastes quite nice but we all agreed that this one was well past eating.

My flipflops broke soon after the rat encounter but it hardly mattered. My feet had become so hard that I scarcely needed shoes and anyway I would be able to buy some more in Mubi. Michel entertained us with the Kapsiki equivalent of an Irish joke as we dropped the final stretch into Duda.

"There was this robber," he said. "He was a Fali. He went into a compound and stole a sack of corn and he was just leaving when someone saw him. The hue and cry went up, but the robber sprinted off and he was getting clean away when somebody had a bright idea. 'Stop him running into the sand,' the person shouted, 'keep him off the sand or he'll escape.' At this the robber instantly changed course for the nearest sand dune and, of course, was caught. Typical Fali."

Our applause did not exactly echo through the hills, but Michel had cheered us up. There were no vehicles expected in Duda that afternoon so we sat in the empty market place to wait, passing the time with sugar cane and tea. It was nearly sunset and egrets were bubbling and croaking in a nearby mango tree when along came an orange tractor with a big blue trailer. It was a Fiat and belonged to the Ministry of Something or Other. Waz and Michel lay in the trailer and I sat on the mudguard, keeping the driver supplied with fags as we bounced towards the town. I was so pleased when we got there that I gave him the awful bottle of scent.

18

Waz had forgotten exactly where his relatives lived, but it was only a temporary hitch and within five minutes of crossing the threshold we were stretched out in a room with a bowl of grade one tuwo, okra soup, bread, tea with condensed milk and so many sleeping mats that we could not shut the door. Waz and Michel set off for a disco but thoughtfully returned with some bog paper for me. There was a standpipe in the compound and I had a splash down with a bucket and a block of pink Camay.

We spent the following day and another night in Mubi doing nothing much at all. Waz's aunt Mairama stuffed us full of rice and meat, and when her five sons came back from school one of them seemed to be continually on duty with a tray of bread and tea. It was marvellous to have all our food arrive without the drudge of fetching wood and water. Mairama's husband was known simply as M.G. and he was the manager of a local cooperative. He showered us with sweets and cigarettes and took me to the drug store where I stocked up on medicines. We also popped round the block to greet Mairama's dying mother. She was extremely old and seemed to be wrinkling up before our eyes.

In the evening all three of us visited Waz's other Mubi aunt, a woman called Hajia. She had a business in the salt trade and had been to Mecca. The sitting room of her house contained neon lights, a new fan on a stand, a big fridge full of soft drinks, and a sofa. The sofa was full of al Haji, a particularly large specimen who was sipping at a Maltex with the expensive sounding rustles that fine rigas make. He wore embroidered slippers and an al Haji cap which must have set him back a few quid too. He was evidently an admirer. Hajia herself was over forty, but unmarried and obviously quite well off. Mairama mentioned that I was also still single. The al Haji looked slightly askance but need not have worried. Mairama was only joking and in any case her sister could have eaten me for breakfast.

Michel had been to Mubi before but never to the cinema. The scene outside the open-air theatre was busy. Music and hard light suffused the darkness, rebounding sharply on glinting bikes in the care of hip swinging minders. Cigarette boys were set up under the trees, and, as usual, the gist of the story was chalked on a blackboard outside the box office. The film itself was a Shaw Brothers production from Hong Kong, which literally kicked off with a market scene. The baddies were bullying the peasantry and scattering their humble stalls. They murdered someone's mother and then raped the hero's girl friend. The goodies leapt into action, confidently predicting that they would "trounce the Warlord's minions," which of course they did, Kung Fuing their way through a long and convoluted plot. The violated heroine let it all out in the final scene. "Kick the aggressor's henchmen," she shouted, and the goodies did that too. Crowd reaction, so essential to a good evening's Kung Fu, was disappointingly subdued but I think Michel quite enjoyed the film.

I had planned to zoom up to Maiduguri for more money, but decided to put this off until we reached Yola, when there would be a further task to perform. Visas for the Cameroons had always been available in border towns but, three months previously, this sensible arrangement had been changed and now there was only one issuing authority, the Cameroonian embassy, about nine hundred miles away down in Lagos. I would have to go there. Michel said that he would be happy to wait for a week or two until I got the paperwork done, and Waz would be going back to Gulak anyway.

Having said goodbye and thank you to Mairama we walked out to the edge of town, threw stones at the vultures on a rubbish tip and stood waiting for a ride back to Duda. I dropped into a patch of maize for five minutes, stroked my beard and watched the sun come up behind a frieze of misty hills. We had no map for the next section and so we took a likely path and followed it up into the steep country south of Duda. The rockiest slopes were wooded with sterculia, a tree whose bark came off in flakes like coloured dandruff. The trunks were a blend of purple, green and grey, with yellow splotches near the crowns. The leaves were shaped like sycamores and the flowers were dull red cups with big white stamens looming out. I collected a few seeds. They were like penicillin capsules, being the size of baked beans with one end shiny black and the other a bright orange.

We crossed the valley of the Yedseram and the road which follows it up from Mubi to the Cameroon border. A Nigerian customs official materialised and very politely checked our gear. He offered us a stick of sugar cane which we sucked as we waded across the river. That night we were put up by a man called Stephanos who asked if Europeans were all of the same nationality.

The large tin of Quaker Oats that we had bought in Mubi died of frequent snacks on the second day, which we spent walking across a rising plateau until we asked someone the way. He turned out to be the local headmaster. Rather than involve himself in a lot of complicated directions he summoned a small boy, gave him the day off and told him to put us on the right track. While young Jacob went off to get his hoop the headmaster plied us with little bananas. Jacob ate most of them as we followed him down a steep path which took us off the plateau. We eventually came to a good vantage point and could see where we were going. Jacob returned home a few pennies richer, and when we turned our heads we saw a happy little speck scampering up the hillside, the hoop over one shoulder and the money, no doubt, still clutched in a disbelieving hand.

A strange vegetable was offered to us in several villages of that district. It looked like a large chunk of flint and it grew under the ground. It was called bokeloje badi in Fulani, which Waz translated as "baboon's balls". It had an equally revolting name in Kapsiki territory where it was known as "leper's yam". It tasted like artichoke roots.

We spent the second night after Mubi under a mango tree. A conference was going on in the darkness of a nearby compound, to which we all listened with interest. Waz gave a running translation from Fulani, which was the local language now that we were in the northern marches of what had once been the emirate of Adamawa. The rather plaintive voice of a girl was to be heard weaving between the sterner tones of two men.

"She wants a new bed," said Waz, "but I think it's only an excuse to leave her husband. He sounds a real creep. He's saying that he has already spent the money that they had for a bed and the girl says he promised her a bed before they married. The other bloke is the girl's father and he keeps telling her to be patient." The father droned on. We learnt that the husband had two other wives, both of whom had very nice beds.

"This often happens," said Waz. "Junior wives sometimes get a raw deal. Gar! The husband's just told her not to always bother her father over everything. He says that since her father only got the price of a donkey when she married she has no right to pester him. What a bastard! He says that you used to be able to try out a wife properly before you took her for keeps, but now women go to school and you can't do that any more. You have to take them on trust. The father's trying to calm things down. Telling everyone to be patient. He's probably worried that he'll have to repay the bride price if the girl leaves. He's some kind of mallam. Oh yes, here we go, he's giving them a bit out of the second sura of the Koran. Now he's reciting the first sura, the Fatiha. In the name of God, most gracious, most merciful and all that. He's saying that it's Friday tomorrow so let God change our hearts and make us

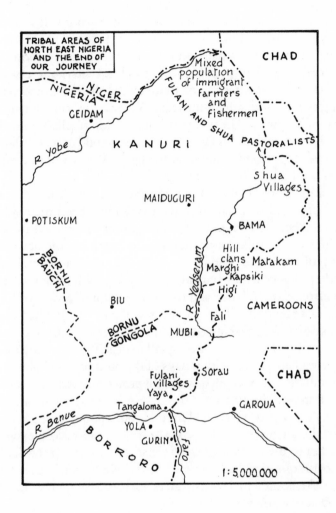

TRIBAL AREAS OF
NORTH EAST NIGERIA
AND THE END OF
OUR JOURNEY

CHAD

NIGER
NIGERIA

GEIDAM

R Yobe

KANURI

Mixed
population
of immigrant
farmers
and
fishermen

FULANI AND SHUA PASTORALISTS

Shua
Villages

MAIDUGURI

• POTISKUM

BAMA

BORNU
BAUCHI

Hill
clans   Matakam
Marghi
Kapsiki
Higi

R Yedseram

BIU

CAMEROONS

BORNU
GONGOLA

Fali

MUBI •

Sorau

Fulani
villages
Yaya •

CHAD

Tangaloma •

GAROUA

R Benue

YOLA •

GURIN •

R Faro

BORRORO

1 : 5,000,000

patient people for the sake of the holy day. Probably won't do much good. She's bound to leave a husband like that in the end."

We joined a dirt road on day three out of Mubi. It took us to a village called Wuro Boka where we plonked in the shade of the empty market place and were gradually surrounded by children. They vanished at two o'clock for afternoon classes, all except for a slender boy of about ten. He had a pointed nose, straight hair and long thin legs. A sleeveless cotton smock hung to his knees. The boy was pale, his skin a lightish tan, not greatly darker than his shoes, which were odd, plastic affairs, both of them trodden down at the heels. Waz asked him why he had not gone off with the others.

"I am a Borroro and I don't go to school," he said.

We had drifted back on to the map, and we left the road at a charred sign which said "Sorau Grazing Reserve—Burning Prohibited". I took a photograph. Fire restricts the development of savannah vegetation, especially in the central and southern zones where burning can be fierce. Many of the trees have fire resistant bark, and the fruits of some species actually require a roasting before the seeds will germinate. I had been shocked by the smoking ruins left in the wake of the first bush fire that I had seen, but was equally surprised to see the bush springing alive again within days of the burn passing. The trees in Sorau district were mostly *Butyrospermum paradoxum*, or shea butter trees. The fruits are the size of bantams' eggs and are widely harvested. They yield an edible oil. The butyrospermums were the shape of young oaks, and they grew close enough together to provide the dreaded tsetse fly with one of the things it most requires in life, namely, shade. We provided the other thing. An adult female tsetse can drink twice her own weight in blood at one go.

All twenty-two species of tsetse carry the trypanosomes which affect animals, and a few carry those which affect man and which give him sleeping sickness. I am not quite sure which sort was biting us in Sorau but it hurt. The nearest thing to a tsetse in England is a horsefly. Luckily for the rest of the world the pest is confined to tropical Africa where its distribution has largely determined where livestock can be raised and where it cannot. One strange fact about the tsetse is that it is viviparous. The female has two small milk glands in her uterus, an almost unheard of thing for an insect to have, and these glands keep the larvae going until they emerge as adults and start cadging free drinks off their fellow creatures. I hate them, especially when I see them cruising away like laden bombers to rest in the bush, but, unlike bombers, they are at their most dangerous when their holds are empty.

The rivers were almost dry but the rocky outcrops made natural swimming holes and the sandy stretches in between were perfect campsites. Fresh tracks of roan antelope and western hartebeeste were kicked into the banks, but disappeared across the iron hard ground except where ash still lingered on like drifts of coal black snow. This was the type of country in which I had worked during my first year as a wildlife officer, when I had been given five hundred square miles of bush to play in. There had been klipspringers high in the rocks, wart hogs down below, and all sorts of other animals in between, and I had had complete freedom to just wander round and watch them. I felt very much at home in the Sorau area, but the country was changing fast, becoming more subdued and steadily more populated.

The villages all had Fulani names which Waz took great pleasure in translating. Most of them were "Wuro" something, which means village or settlement. There was Wuro Tapere, meaning "Magician's Village", and a place called "Cattle Drive". Several settlements were named after their founders, and some had names like "Fish" or "Chicken". A few names were inspired by the geography. "Stream Town", "Deep Place" and "Forest" were examples. Many villages were very small but most had an enormous pile of wood ash at some central spot where the Koranic school met. Classes were given in the evening and in the early morning and it was the duty of the pupils to maintain the fire by which they worked. The sound of children chanting their verses well into the night and in the darkness of pre-dawn is one of my enduring memories of bush village life.

A baboon barked a harsh farewell from the last outcrop as we emerged on to the plain of the Tiel river, a tributary of the Benue. We were only a thousand feet above sea level and it was hot again, although the nights were becoming cooler as December approached its second week. On the day before we reached the Benue we stopped at a place called Wuro Yaya, and we made camp beneath a gigantic bombax tree, each of us in our own little compartment in the buttresses. As the evening drew on the head of each household set a bowl of food before us. We had six lots altogether, and a bowl of milk. We couldn't eat it all, but took a handful from each bowl as was polite. The people were "settled" Fulanis from the Republic of Niger. They had come down to Nigeria because of a drought and had eventually reached Yaya. They had simply piled all their belongings into a Mammy Wagon and headed south. They had had no maps and no idea of where they were. They just knew that the land was good enough to farm and, as they said, God had decided when they should stop. The local authority had not objected, and they had been living round the bombax tree for the past three years.

The whole area was stiff with Borroro. The Benue lowlands offer them excellent grazing, especially in the dry season when other places get used up. The young men were particularly striking. Waz said that he thought they were hermaphrodites (I think he meant transvestites), because they took such enormous care over their appearance, especially their hair which tended to be plaited in extremely complex ways then bound with silver wire.

We stopped beside a stream to ask the way of a slender, almost fragile Borroro woman in a black wrapper. All three of us had a wash and while we were drying ourselves the old girl swiped our soap. It was all we had and it took some time to get it back. Waz eventually told her that I had come to improve the water supply and wouldn't be able to do so if I weren't clean.

210

He had developed blisters, his first since the Polder episode, and we were having problems hitting the river. A waterway the size of the Benue should not have been too hard to find, but it was eluding us. Village after village just had to be "it", and wasn't, but we retained a sense of humour.

"I hope you two recognise the sea when you get there," said Waz. We had now come far enough to be able to laugh about our past blunders. Waz stopped to adjust his laces. "Really," he said, "you could say that we got into the routine of being lost from the first day." Eventually we reached a village that was indeed "it". Its name was Tangaloma and it stood right on the river's edge. We stared across the half mile of flat water. The sun hung cool above the stillness, shades of red and gold cast down across the surface. Something touched the cue of silent colour and the sun dropped quickly out of sight. A canoe was slipping towards a broken section of the bank, where other dug-outs were moored, floating like a hand of slim bananas on the dark, scum bobbing, mirror snake of river.

"Made it," I said.

"Five hundred miles," said Waz, which was about how far we had walked, but we still had six or seven hundred to go, with some pretty remote country ahead of us. Michel didn't say anything. He just pursed his lips and spat into the water. The white blob hardly moved.

The Tangaloma people were Kabbaras from Sokoto in the north-west, and had been living on the Benue for the past fifteen years, fishing the river and farming the rich flood plain. It was too late to cross that evening and so the headman kindly made a hut available to us. We had run out of sugar and cigarettes, and were just falling into a mosquito ridden sleep when a Toyota drew up outside. What sounded like a Brazilian football commentary burst from the four loudspeakers mounted on the cab. I thought it was some political speech or perhaps a sermon, but it wasn't. The chap was selling Lux beauty soap.

The trip across the river was quite a laugh. Michel and I paddled, and the boatman steered from the back. Waz held on tight and hoped that we would not tip over. The south bank turned out to be an extensive beach, on which thousands of cattle were just waking up. They were gathered in herds round the beehive shaped huts of their Borroro owners who were stretching and yawning in the cool dawn air. Some men stood muffled in their shawls, their prayer beads hanging from their fingers as they contemplated the coming day, while others were releasing calves from tethers dug into the sand.

Extricating ourselves from the jungly clutches of the south bank was a problem but we finally did it and twenty miles later we reached the town of Gurin. The intervening country had been flat and boring, much of it planted down to rice. At first we had watched the herons and the cormorants but as we left the river behind we just put our heads down and walked. Michel was very good at it. He drank and ate very little during the day, and did not smoke, although he was a little chagrined to find that these Adamawa people did not make beer. Waz's ankle was giving trouble and he hitched a lift for the last couple of miles, a great relief to Michel and me because we also dumped our gear in the truck that stopped to pick Waz up. We were both completely buggered by the time we reached Gurin and lurched dazedly to the lorry park where Waz was waiting. We drunk mugs of weak Ovaltine at an "hotel" and scoffed oily doughnuts out of brown paper. I managed not to fall off the bench. We also had a dollop of pounded yam which was a mark of how far south we had progressed.

19

There were thirty or forty miles to go before the next stretch of interesting country which was called the Atlantika Mountains, and beyond that lay the Mambilla Plateau which I was eagerly looking forward to crossing. First we needed a good rest, and I also had to go to Lagos for my visa. We caught a minibus from Gurin to Yola where we stayed the night with Waz's uncle Idrissu, the husband of Mrs. Madame. I liked him. He had a sparkling sense of humour and told us all about Lagos where he had been a senator. He had delighted in playing the dumb northerner. People in Lagos were, apparently, under the impression that the bush began at the city limits and that a place like Yola was Ultima Thule. Was it true, quite educated people had asked Idrissu, that cattle which fetched a thousand naira in the city were sold for ten naira each up there?

"I told them No," said Idrissu, lapsing into his hilarious pidgin, "no be so at all. Say you no go buy um o! How you wantum make you catchum for de bush go sendum dere for Lagos. De bif be free dere for de bush, jus Good Lord help you gettum." He did a brilliant send-up of Lagos shop girls too.

"It's amazing down there," he said, "I wrapped a really enormous turban round my head once and waddled into a supermarket like a real old al Haji. They sent a girl round the shop with me. I kept asking her what the things were and she thought I was a real bush man. I tried to pay her, but she said no, pay at the desk and I said 'Wonderful'. So I go to the desk and started bargaining for everything and they say 'No bargaining, everything fixed price,' and I said 'Wonderful' again. They put all the stuff in a box and they were giggling and laughing at me. So I was just about to leave and I handed the box over to the girl and I said, 'OK, thank you, deliver this to my office will you, 11th floor, Congress House.' "

That night we heard the news that John Lennon had been shot. This made me feel a little older, and sad enough to cry. The harmattan had descended on the country, turning everything cobwebby, and we drove through it back to Gulak, where I dumped the gear, collected my mail and headed for Maiduguri. An empty cattle truck pulled up and I hopped into the front while a stack of new pots was put on the back.

The cab was challengingly stark. I lowered myself on to an oily plank which had been jammed across the passenger side, and we juddered forward. There must be some mistake, I felt. Had pneumatic drills been slipped between the springs? The noise was clinically dangerous. I shut my eyes. We could have been freewheeling down the Golan Heights in an abandoned tank. I say "we" because there were two others in the cab. They were both called John and they came from Anambra state down in the south. Big John was the "driver". He kept the wheel between his knees which left his hands free for changing gear and rolling joints for which he used the sports page of *The New Nigerian*. He looked up from time to time and frowned at the windscreen, but he could not see much through the fog, and in any case his eyes were red as drains. It was Little John who did most of the work. One of his duties was to throw out the "seat" every time we stopped. He did this in order to reconnect the battery. His other job was to take charge of the "key", a six-inch nail which the laid-back John would have doubtless lost.

We stopped in Bama to offload the pots. Big J was on his way to Maiduguri for cattle, but augmented his pay with small private loads when he was travelling unladen. His salary was a hundred naira a month plus twenty naira a trip for his expenses.

"Not much," he said. We were sitting on some old oil drums watching Little John unloading the pots with a couple

214

of labourers. The sports page crinkled as Big John inhaled. His eyes became even redder. The monosyllabic haze in which he drove, combined with the noise level in the cab, inhibited conversation and Little John hardly opened his mouth either because, unusually for an Anambran, he did not speak much English.

"I no de go for school," he said. "Our teesha die."

We pulled out of Bama, grating through the gears until we were doing about sixty miles an hour. A large and stupid ram was standing in the road. The lorry was closing rapidly and the ram panicked. It then did a very silly thing indeed. Instead of running left or right to safety, it went for the kamikazi option and began to race forward along the road. Even had it got up full steam it was doomed. Its top speed was nowhere near sixty. The poor thing was hardly out of first when it was overtaken by twenty yards of completely unstoppable truck.

I made sympathetic noises and Little John looked back, but there was absolutely no reaction from Big John. He hadn't even touched the brakes, nor had he changed course. The ram had been a goner, and stopping for a post mortem would have involved endless hassles over liability with the crowd which was bound to materialise. The animal would be despatched very quickly if it were not already dead. The roadsiders were certain to be Muslims and they liked their meat to be kosher; that is, with a slit throat and a prayer. Big John drove calmly on. I began to wonder if he had noticed the ram at all when at last he turned his head. His eyes blinked like geraniums.

"Ah," he said, by way of an elegy. "This Nigeria." He sighed. "We are, er . . . ." There was a long pause and much deliberate thought. "We are . . . disting . . ." His voice trailed off and he turned his eyes back to the road. I thought that that was it, but he suddenly took a deep breath and, very slowly, he spoke. He seemed to be addressing the dead speedometer.

"This Nigeria," he said. "We are going forward. But We Are Still A Developing Country."

He then struggled with a bottle in his jacket pocket. Having got the top off he took a long swig at the maroon coloured liquid. It looked like Ribena, but was in fact neat Campari.

I was three parts pissed by the time we reached Maiduguri. The headlights were doing battle with both dust and darkness. I hailed a cab, spent the night with my friends and met the Johns as arranged the following afternoon at the cattle market. Big John had planned to leave for Lagos that night but there had been some kind of hitch and I began to look for another truck. A couple of dozen thirty-five tonners were lined up to receive their cargoes, which were driven up concrete ramps from the holding pens with much violence and blasphemy. The scene was not dissimilar to the Sussex market places on whose railings I had perched as a boy, except that the cows were far bigger and they were being carried in open trucks.

I went down the line, knocking on cab doors and asking for Kano. Eventually the driver of a new Fiat told me to get in.

"How much?" I asked.

"Just get in," he said. His name was Sunday and he was an Ashanti from Ghana. His mate was a Nigerian called Felix and they were going to Lagos. There was a bed across the back of the cab from which I enjoyed a bird's eye view of the glorious traffic jam which had developed just outside the market. The recently formed traffic police were whistling enthusiastically. They wore white gloves and distinctive orange shirts and were entirely ineffective. They were known as the Yellow Peril. We escaped them and rolled out of town at sunset.

Sunday drove all night, and, despite six police checks, we reached Kano at dawn but we didn't stop. The police checks cost about two naira a time and usually consisted of a couple of battered oil drums in the road, a machine pistol and a couple of constables standing in the headlights. A superior would usually be lurking around somewhere to make sure that the constables handed over the loot. If you didn't offer a little contribution you found yourself parked for the night, which was not good for the cattle. I made some remark about the frequency of the police stops.

"Used to be much worse than this," said Sunday. "It wasn't

just the police. It got to a stage outside Lagos recently when there would be a whole line of them—Police, Army, Yellow Peril, Customs, and then the Air Force decided it wasn't getting any of the action so it joined in too. Head of State cut it down and now it's back to just the police."

We bowled south through the harmattan. Sunday and Felix changed over every four or five hours and although we couldn't see much countryside there were plenty of wrecks to stimulate the imagination, about one every mile and a half on average. Just before we crossed the Niger there was an especially good one with half a dozen railway carriages and eight big lorries in a twisted embrace. The river itself slipped out of the mist in a great ochre coloured sweep, slithered under the pylons of the bridge and vanished into the gloom.

At ten on the second night there was a tap on the cab window. One of the cows was dying and the dealer wanted to stop. He was a wizened little man smothered in yards of cheesecloth against the night air and with two labourers was travelling perched above the cows on a platform of canvas and sticks which was lashed to the lorry's superstructure. Sunday nodded.

We swept past a nice fresh capsize, a vehicle carrier loaded with white Peugot 504s. The crew had marked off the disaster with branches and were squatting round a fire. We didn't stop, but Sunday mentioned it to someone when we pulled up to deal with the cow in the next township. The usual procedure was to sell sick cows en route, because no one would buy them once they had actually died, but I do not know what the form was with Peugeots. The nearer one got to Lagos the weaker the cows became, and the locals knew this very well. It was late, but a prospective buyer arrived within a couple of minutes and offered 180 naira. There were muffled "albarka"s from the back, standard refusals of a first offer. The cowmen were trying to get the sick animal to its feet, hazardous work in the crush of the other twenty-six head on board. The lorry "boy", balding and in glasses, also travelling in the back, translated from Kanuri to Yoruba. The offer was increased to a paltry

217

190 naira, the asking price reduced to 320, but no deal was reached.

The cow was actually still alive when we got to Lagos despite a couple of hours' rest on the approach motorway. It was too early for dealing to start and so we had stopped for some sleep. I woke to a furious tirade. A lorry had spilled its load of cocoa and the driver was refusing to go back for it. He appeared to be entirely unconcerned but the owner of the cocoa had arrived and was beside himself. Sunday wisely refused a request to talk to the cocoa driver. The owner was apopleptic.

"Dis driba, he no de know but he play wid life," he shrieked.

The cattle market turned out to be a spare bit of land at a motorway intersection, really nothing more than a large traffic island. Yellow minibuses circled us like Indians on the war path. One actually bit the dust before our very eyes, but was quickly surrounded by a posse of the Yellow Peril. It was still only seven o'clock, but other trucks had started to roll in, and down their tailgates staggered Lagos's Sunday lunch. The area was completely unfenced but after thirty-six hours and a thousand miles with no food or water the cows were too bemused to wander far. Groups of men were huddled together in the haze, waiting for the buyers to arrive, but I could not linger, and Sunday flagged a taxi down. He told the driver not to rip me off and I was whisked into the city about which I had heard so much.

Sunday and Felix had, of course, spent hours telling me to be careful. Waz had issued stern instructions and my brother, who had worked in the city for a while, had also told me various horror stories. With considerable trepidation I reached the Y.M.C.A., and it was something of an anticlimax to find that not only was a room available very cheaply, but that some very nice people were also staying there. It was a Sunday and my room mate, a journalist on the Lagos *Observer*, invited me to divine service. We strolled over to Josephine's Eating House for a late breakfast. My insides had settled and I was feeling lucky. I had thought about swallowing my valuables as a safety measure, but British passports make an awkward morsel and I stuck to my usual system of a pocket sewn to the inside of my trousers. Just where I stitch my secret compartment would be telling, but it seems to work.

I had a day to kill and wandered round the National Museum. Three riot policemen were also perusing the nation's heritage. They were fully armed and clattered round the exhibits in their protective gear and boots. Perhaps they had not noticed the cloakroom. I came across a cricket match near the city centre. The players were mostly Indians, although the scorer was a Nigerian. Everyone was immaculately dressed. I also wandered into the sailing club where a help-yourself cold buffet was on offer, so I did. The trick was to look as if you belonged and I must say the lunch was delicious. Being a jolly jack tar was one thing, but successful mingling at the polo club was quite another. I had discovered the place by following the beautifully groomed ponies as they were being trotted up from the police barracks just behind the Y.M.C.A., but, having spotted the uniformed attendants at the entrance, I confined myself to the car park and watched over the railings. I have played polo a couple of times courtesy of the Maiduguri club and a friend who lent me his motor-cycle crash helmet. I found hitting the ball extremely difficult but it is a most exhilarating sport and if I become rich before I ossify I shall take it up, but probably not in Lagos, where Sunday is games afternoon for a rather small number of citizens only.

I was outside the Cameroonian embassy at eight sharp and was told that my application for a visa would be processed and ready for collection at two. I smiled knowingly.

"Today?"

"Yes, today afternoon." I did not believe it, but I was wrong.

In the meantime I shot through a couple of supermarkets from which Christmas carols were blaring across the streets. I bought a box of crackers for my Maiduguri friends and blew my mind on chocolate and ice-cream. I made a mental note to congratulate Idrissu who had been absolutely spot on with his imitation of the shop girls. On the way back to the embassy I took in the Cathedral Church of Christ, which, being a Monday, was almost empty. White faces beamed down from the stained glass windows and there were long lists of the Reverends who had died in service carved on marble tablets. The church had been founded in 1869 when West Africa had been the Passchendaele of missionary endeavour.

I stood in amazement at the embassy gates. It was five past two o'clock. My passport contained the precious visa. I had not been robbed and I was ready to go. The journey back to Maiduguri took twenty-four hours by long distance taxi. I slept most of the way but woke up when we stopped for petrol and reversed into a storm drain. We stood around while the garage staff lifted the car out. A fellow passenger produced a gramophone record from his bag and passed it round.

"It's E.M.I.," he said.

"Oh yes," said another, examining the label. "This is the well known E.M.I. He was an electrical salesman, yes, and now he is producing his own records. He even sings his own records. He works very hard in disting, um, electrician industry and now he is a rich man." This information was imparted with absolute conviction. The record was returned to the owner.

"You see," he said, showing us the label, "made in Nigeria." Our man on the pop scene frowned.

"Perhaps this Made in Nigeria records don't last as long as, er, as . . ." He paused for inspiration. It struck from an unexpected quarter. "As Jim Reeves," the man said with a rush. I smothered a surge of manic laughter. The man went on, oblivious of my agony. "Yes," he said, "you can play this Jim Reeves so many times and they never wear out."

I was feeling a little dazed with all the whizzing about of the past week and was glad to finally reach Gulak. I arrived on the afternoon of 17 December with a singing head. I thought that I might have caught a touch of 'flu. Much to my relief Michel was still keen and completely ready to go. His wife had come down to say goodbye and to collect an advance on Michel's wages, since, if all went according to plan, she would not be seeing him again until we returned from Victoria. The next stage of the journey was about to start and the following day we would travel back to Gurin and take up the trail once more.

Unfortunately my temperature increased during the night, and I assumed that I had caught malaria. I lay in Waz's room in Gulak for two more days and got worse and worse. Waz eventually transferred me to the compound of some Swiss missionaries who lived about a mile away and to whom I am eternally grateful. I sank into glorious oblivion for ten days, interrupted only twice. The first time was by a large hypodermic driven by a small nun who also thought that I had malaria. The second time was by an American doctor who was sure that I did not. His theory was hepatitis, and unfortunately he was right. It would be at least two months, if not three or four, until I would be strong enough to continue, he said, and he was right about that too. One major consolation was that my insides were much better, because even walking to the bog was quite a feat.

Four weeks later I was well enough to crawl on to a plane for home. I must say I felt pretty depressed, but I cheered up in the Cairo transit lounge. The place was crawling with cats, and the poor chap who took the chair opposite me slowly discovered that he had sat right in a fresh dollop of moggy do's. I felt awfully sorry for him but there was nothing I could do to help. We all have our problems, I thought. My brother met me at Heathrow and he drove me back to Hastings. We went via Staines, but we didn't say much to each other as I was again in the back feeling grotty. The border project was over.

I had not, to use a trenchant phrase, achieved my aim, but in the following months of convalescence I discovered that assimilation can be at least the equal of achievement. Journeys so often become just a list of miles and mountain tops—and to worry unduly about the menu is often to miss the meal altogether. It struck me that my own road had spoken most effectively when I had been least demanding of its voice. Though far removed from the sea I had, when concentrating less on listening than on hearing, in some way sensed an ocean. A certain quality had laced the air in these rare moments. Breathing deeply, I had found myself upon an open strand, my footprints washed by the elusive tides as I had wandered slowly on, along the beach of morning.

Further Reading

A great many books and articles were consulted. The main ones are listed below.

Abraham, R. C., *A Dictionary of the Hausa Language*, University of London Press, 1962

Barth, Heinrich, *Travels and Discoveries in North and Central Africa*, Longman, 1857

Beek, W. A., van, *The Kapsiki of Mogode*, unpublished ms.

Calvert, A. F., *Nigeria and its Tin Fields*, Edward Stanford, 1912

Clapperton, Commander H., *Journal of a Second Expedition into the Interior of Africa*, John Murray, 1829

Cohen, R., *The Kanuri of Bornu*, North Western University Press, 1967

Connah, G., *Three Thousand Years in Africa: Man and his Environment in the Lake Chad Region of Nigeria*, Cambridge University Press, 1981

Crozier, Brigadier F. P., *Five Years Hard*, Cape, 1932

Denham, Dixon, *Narrative of Travels and Discoveries in North and Central Africa, 1822–4*, London, 1826

Gardi, R., *Kirdi*, Paris, 1957

Gardi, R., *Mandara*, Zurich, 1956

Gauthier, J., *Les Fali*, Oosterhout, 1969

Hutchinson, J. and Dalziel, J. M., *Flora of West Tropical Africa*, London, 1931–6

Johnston, H. A. S., *The Fulani Empire of Sokoto*, Oxford University Press, 1967

Kirk-Greene, A., *Adamawa Past and Present*, Oxford University Press, 1958

Kirk-Greene, A., *The Kingdom of Sukur, Nigerian Field*, 1960

Kirk-Greene, A., with Kraft, C. H., *Teach Yourself Hausa*, Hodder and Stoughton, 1973

Kirk-Greene, A., with Sassoon, C., *The Cattle People of Fulani Nigeria*, Oxford University Press, 1959

Lewis, M. (ed.), *Islam in Tropical Africa*, Oxford University Press, 1966

Meeren, A. G. L., van der, *A Socio-Anthropological Analysis of the Fisheries of Lake Chad*, unpublished

Nash, T. A. M., *Africa's Bane—the Tsetse Fly*, Collins, 1969

Nasr, S. H., *Islamic Life and Thought*, George Allen and Unwin, 1981

Praed, C. W. Mackworth and Grant, C. H. B., *Birds of West Central and Western Africa*, Longman, 1970

Schultze, A. (trans. from the German, Benton, P. A.), *The Sultanate of Bornu*, F. Cass, 1968

Sikes, S., *Lake Chad*, Eyre Methuen, 1972

Stenning, D. J., *Savannah Nomads*, Oxford University Press, 1959

Trimingham, J. S., *History of Islam in West Africa*, Oxford University Press, 1962

Tuchman, B., *A Distant Mirror*, Macmillan, 1979

Vaughan, J. H., *Religion and World View of the Marghi, Ethnology*, 3:4, 1964

White, S., *Descent from the Hills*, John Murray, 1961

White, S., *Dan Bwana*, John Murray, 1959